**DOCUMENTS AND SOURCES
IN ARCHITECTURE
VOLUME I**

**LAUGIER
AN ESSAY ON ARCHITECTURE**

AN
ESSAY
ON
ARCHITECTURE

by
MARC-ANTOINE LAUGIER

Translated and with an introduction by
Wolfgang and Anni Herrmann

HENNESSEY & INGALLS, INC.
LOS ANGELES   1977

Copyright © 1977 by Hennessey & Ingalls, Inc.
Printed in the United States of America

Library of Congress Cataloging in Publication Data

Laugier, Marc-Antoine, 1713–1769.
  An essay on architecture.

  (Documents and sources in architecture; no. 1)
  Translation of Essai sur l'architecture.
  1. Architecture—Early works to 1800.   I. Title.
NA2515.L2913   720   75-28448
ISBN 0-912158-92-1

CONTENTS

Laugier's
ESSAY ON ARCHITECTURE

The *Essai sur l'architecture*, presented here in an English translation, appeared in the bookshops of Paris in the early spring of 1753. The first comment we have on the book was given six months earlier, however. The publisher, as required by law, had submitted it to the censor, who appreciated its quality—*plein de goust et de génie* he calls it—but thought that the author had been too outspoken in his critical remarks and that some moderation in this respect was called for. Therefore, before granting the *approbation* he had a word with the author or, more likely, with the publisher or a friend acting as go-between for a writer determined to remain anonymous.[1] Reading the book in its published form, one finds it difficult to believe that the censor succeeded in softening the peremptory tone in which it was written.

The anonymity of its author was maintained for a little while. At this time, when *philosophes* entertained what were considered to be subversive ideas, all literary production was subjected not only to a comparatively tolerant censorship but also to a strict surveillance by the police who, of course, were taking a special interest in books published anonymously. In this case they did not rest until they had found out—and it

[1] Paris, Bibl. Nat. MS. fond franç. anc. 22139, fol. 142.

did not take them long—that the author was a Jesuit priest by the name of Laugier. They may have concluded from the decisive and uncompromising tenor of the book that, as his literary critics also assumed, it was the first publication of a young man, and they may have been surprised—and perhaps relieved—to discover that it was the work of a man who by then had passed forty, a mature age for a time when life expectancy was half of what it is now.

Marc-Antoine Laugier was a Provençal, born on January 22, 1713, in Manosque, where the Laugiers belonged to the upper strata of the bourgeoisie. When he was fourteen it was decided that he should become a priest, a profession normally chosen for the younger son of a family, and that the Jesuit order was the appropriate one. He first entered the college at nearby Avignon from where three years later, having completed his novitiate, he was transferred for further studies and the final four years' course in theology to other colleges of the Lyons Province—to Lyons itself, to Besançon, Marseilles, Nîmes and Alès. Although during all these years theological instructions took up the major part of his studies, he had at the same time the advantage of partaking in the excellent and wide-ranging public education for which the Jesuits were justly renowned. Already he was interested in architecture and its theoretical aspect. While he lived in Nîmes in 1742, he examined the newly discovered antique fountain there. Ten years later when writing the *Essai*, he remembered seeing "fragments of an extremely bizarre cornice" which he characterized as being "of bad taste almost without parallel."[2] The antique temple in the same town, the so-called *Maison Carrée*, was greatly admired by him and in fact became an important stimulus to the development of his architectural theory; but his enthusiasm for the simplicity of its architecture did not stop him from examining it in detail so that when dealing in his book with the correct form of the

[2]See p. 58.

Corinthian Order he still remembers the "peculiar position" of the modillions which, he points out, "are wrongly placed" there.[3]

It may have been due to a natural aptitude for preaching that he was transferred at the age of thirty from the Lyons Province to the House of the Jesuits in Paris. His first impression when entering Paris did not come up to his expectation; the description he gives in the *Essai* of a stranger's reaction to the miserable way the capital of France presented itself was, no doubt, that of his own reaction and of his own disappointment.[4] However, in other respects Paris had much to offer him and in the end even became the center of events that caused the decisive turning point of his life.

On February 2, 1745, a few months after his arrival, he took his final vows. We learn that two years later and again the following year he gave the Lenten sermons in St. Sulpice, a church which stylistically embodied everything that was distasteful to him. His preaching, backed by "fine looks and a deep voice,"[5] must have been notable, since he was chosen to deliver in the same year the four advent sermons in Fontainebleau in the presence of the king. They were, no doubt, oratorically outstanding, but as to content do not seem to have been out of the ordinary. This, however, was quite different six years later when, during Lent, he preached in the Chapel of Versailles, again in the presence of the king and the whole Court. This time, "everybody speaks" about the Jesuit who "delivered altogether fanatical sermons."[6] That they "made a great stir," as one of the courtiers noted in his diary,[7] was only natural since Laugier referred in them directly and with great vehemence to the political situation of

[3]See p. 57.
[4]See p. 126.
[5]Duc de Luynes, *Mémoires*, ed. Didot, 1860 ff., X, p. 228.
[6]d'Argenson, *Journal et Mémoires du Marquis d'Argenson*, ed. Rathery for the *Societé de l'Hist. de France*, 1859 ff., VIII, pp. 250, 265 f.
[7]de Luynes, *loc. cit.*

the day in which the Court, the Church, Parliament and the People were openly confronting each other with the Jesuits trying to exploit the confused situation and thus divert the widespread attacks directed against them as the alleged power behind the throne. Laugier "thundered against the amusements of the king," admonishing him to be more concerned in future with the defense of the Church, to punish the unbelievers who were the "authors of the revolt" and to suppress Parliament, which was out to destroy religion.[8] He must certainly have acted on the orders of his superiors when he used the pulpit for political ends, but since he was unable to comply with Cardinal de Soubise's request to submit his sermon beforehand because, as he said, he spoke "extempore," it is possible that, carried away, he overstepped the guidelines prescribed to him. However that may be, a few days after his last sermon on Easter Sunday 1754, Laugier was ordered by his superior to return to the province to which within the Society he belonged and enter again the main college in Lyons. If his sermons had already caused considerable excitement among the entourage of the king, the disciplinary action taken by the Society at a moment of social and political unrest made Laugier's case notorious. A pamphlet was published purporting to base its day-by-day account of what had led to Laugier's banishment on firsthand information, but since the author's main concern was obviously to exploit the affair fully so as to make it into an effective weapon in his fight against the Jesuits, his account is suspect and of value only as showing the general interest in Laugier's fate. It is no wonder that the police were once more interested in him, the inspector ending his note by saying "the Jesuits have just sent Father Laugier back to his Province. . . . This poor Jesuit has been completely taken by surprise by this catastrophy."[9] In any case, Laugier com-

[8] d'Argenson, *loc. cit.*
[9] Paris, Bibl. Nat. MS. fond franç. anc. 22159, fol. 34.

plied with the order and returned to Lyons. Since in December of the following year he was entrusted with the honorable task of delivering the funeral speech for the Prince de Dombes, the great protector of the Jesuits, and since furthermore the title page of the fine edition in which the oration was published in 1756 names him as "R. P. Laugier de la Compagnie de Jésus, Prédicateur du Roi," it seems unlikely that the order given to Laugier was meant as a punishment or that he himself felt a resentment on that score. Conflict there was, but of a different nature; it must be looked for within his own personality.

In the years preceding the events just outlined, Laugier's literary activity was remarkable. During 1752 he put the final touch to his *Essai*, which was published anonymously because, as he said in the preface to the second edition, if his name had been known—and by that he meant his status as a Jesuit priest—it could have given rise to prejudices unfavorable to him. According to information received by the police, even the Society itself was unaware of the author's identity until the summer when the success of the work was assured. Laugier then wrote a short article under his own name in reply to specific criticisms raised in a lengthy review of the *Essai* that had appeared in a Journal close to the Jesuits. The book was, undoubtedly, very successful. It was reviewed in all the important journals of the day and by all the leading literary critics. Laugier was pleasantly surprised that it had found "favor among the many."[10] This reception, according to two important reviews, was due to the realization that here at last was a book on architectural theory that the laymen could read "with the pleasure with which one reads light literature" and "almost at a sitting without being bored,"[11] The beauty of his style of writing was praised; it

[10]See p. 148.
[11]*Mercure de France*, May 1753, p. 104; *Journal de Trevoux*, May 1753, p. 1073.

was described as "always vivid; elegant and harmonious."[12] All this praise must have encouraged him to try his pen on other subject matters which, in fact, comprised, next to architecture, the figurative arts as well as music. In autumn 1753 he published, again anonymously, a critical review of the *Salon* of that year in the form of a letter addressed to the Marquis de Vence, and early the following year a pamphlet, still anonymously, entitled *Apologie de la musique française contre M. Rousseau,* thereby joining the so-called *guerre des bouffons* that had been waged among music lovers following Rousseau's assertion of the superiority of Italian music. Already by the end of 1753, Laugier was reported to be preparing a new enlarged edition of the *Essai,* a work that must have taken up much of his time during the following months—including those weeks in Lent when he delivered his "fanatical" sermons. Arising out of this preparatory work he wrote, when already back in Lyons, a reply to a highly critical review by a well-known architect which had appeared in the *Mercure de France* in July, a reply that he had reprinted as an addendum to the second edition. Laugier evidently took a paramount interest in aesthetic problems and may have found it difficult to let his duties as a member of the Society of Jesus take precedence over his literary inclinations. The conflict of loyalties must have preyed on his mind from the moment the favorable reception of the *Essai* opened the prospect of a new and more congenial occupation; so it seems credible that someone who moved in the literary circles of Paris and was always well informed was told already in December 1753 of certain indications that "P. Laugier will soon be counted among the number of ex-Jesuits who are of such great credit to literature."[13] The events which finally forced him to leave Paris just turned the scale. He felt, as his

[12]*Journal des Scavans,* June 1753, pp. 432 ff.
[13]Grimm, *Correspondance littéraire. . . . ,* ed. Tourneaux, Paris, 1877 ff., II, p. 306.

literary friends reportedly told him, that he was wasted in the province and that only the capital offered the right arena for talented people.

By the end of 1754 at the latest but probably earlier, Laugier took the decisive step. He asked La Curne de Sainte-Palaye, an eminent scholar of Provencal language and literature, to write to Cardinal Passionei, the liberal-minded dignitary of the Roman Church known for his hostile attitude towards the Jesuits, and appeal for his help in obtaining papal permission to leave the order. It turned out to be a long, and for Passionei troublesome, procedure. The whole of 1755 was taken up in submitting evidence and finding an order willing to accept Laugier once the *Bref de transtation* was granted by the Pope. At last, in March 1756, the successful conclusion to the whole business was achieved. Passionei, relieved, announced this in a personal letter addressed to "P. Laugier, Ex-Jesuit," saying how pleased he was to have secured him the peace of mind which he imagined absolutely necessary.[14] Laugier belonged now to the Priory of the Benedictine Abbey St. Vaast de Moreuil in the diocese of Amiens; but this, as Passionei himself indicated, was purely a matter of form. From then on he was known as l'Abbé Laugier.

He was now his own master and soon moved to Paris, where he took his lodgings in a small street in the Marais. He was free but without the material support which the Society had so far provided. Income from his literary work would have been quite insufficient, so he had to look for some post giving adequate remuneration to allow him to occupy his free time with the pursuit of those things which attracted him most—art criticism and historical research. Having already made a name for himself by the two editions of the *Essai* and his other writings, and enjoying the patronage of men as influential as Lacurne de Sainte-Palaye, who had just been

[14]Paris, Bibl. Nat. MS. Coll. Moreau No. 1567, fols. 14-72.

elected to the *Académie*, the Comte de Vence and, no doubt, other society members, he was in a better position than many other *hommes de lettres* whose ranks he had now joined. He succeeded in obtaining the post of editor of the official *Mercure de France*, a position which he held for two or three years. Although the editor took his directions from Malesherbes, the head of the department controlling the press, and although much of his work consisted only in collecting official announcements, his position nevertheless brought him into contact with powerful people in the various ministries. It is therefore not surprising to hear that when the Marquis de Bausset was appointed ambassador to the Elector of Cologne, he chose as his secretary Laugier, "one of the oldest protégés" of the Duc de Choiseuil, the Minister of Foreign Affairs (as Laugier himself reminds Choiseuil in one of his dispatches from Cologne). By the beginning of 1760 Laugier was in Cologne and, since the ambassador could not take up his post until later, was in charge of the embassy for the next five months. A great number of his dispatches are preserved, the most intriguing—at least for us today—being those in which he asks for instructions on what action to take about the suspiciously prolonged stay in Cologne of a dubious character by the name of Giacomo Casanova! Three years later, Laugier was again in charge of the embassy while Bausset made preparations in Paris for his new appointment to the Court of St. Petersburg. The intention was for Laugier to accompany the ambassador to Russia, but by August 1763 Bausset changed his mind, for "private reasons," and took somebody else with him.[15]

Laugier remained in Paris where he moved into a more fashionable quarter of the town, close to the *Bibliothèque du Roi*. There, with some of the furniture lent to him by wealthy

[15] The dispatches are preserved in Paris, Archives Ministère Affaires Etrangères, Corr. Pol. Cologne, No. 98.

patrons, he occupied a small *appartement* of three rooms where over the years he collected a small library of about five hundred books. He could now live, comfortably it seems, on his income deriving from pensions he must have been granted as former editor of the *Gazette de France* and possibly also for the years spent in the diplomatic service, and on the remuneration he received for his numerous books. Thus for the first time he could follow his inclinations and devote all his time to literary work.

He completed his most ambitious writing, the *Histoire de la République de Venise*, the first volume of which had already come out in 1758 while the last, the twelfth, was not published until almost ten years later. This great work and, of course, his fame as author of the *Essai* had already brought him the honor of being elected member of the Academies of Angers, Lyons, and Marseilles, all three in quick succession during the summer of 1760 while he was in Cologne. The history of Venice was not so well received as the *Essai*, though it remained in France the standard work on Venetian history for the next fifty years and ran in its Italian translation into three editions.

His main interest, however, centered around the arts, architecture in particular. By 1759 he had worked out a detailed scheme for a journal devoted exclusively to the discussion of every aspect of the arts, of architecture, painting and sculpture as well as of the applied arts, giving information on artists and reviewing books dealing with the arts. Laugier quite rightly felt that such a novel and ambitious undertaking needed official backing and submitted the plan for the journal, to be called *L'état des arts en France*, to the Marquis de Marigny who as *Directeur des Bâtiments* was in fact responsible for the organization of all the arts. Unfortunately, nothing came of it, mainly due to the hostile attitude of the artists, who were alarmed about the trend towards complete emancipation of art criticism. Thus, Laugier was prevented from pioneering what would have become the first art periodical in history.

He must, therefore, have been all the more satisfied when the Chapter of Amiens, wishing to renovate the choir of the Cathedral, consulted him, the amateur. They had approached him before and had carried out some of his suggestions, but had now started on a more ambitious scheme and commissioned not only a number of well-known artists but also Laugier to submit a plan for the complete redecoration of the choir. This plan is not preserved, but Laugier, who at this time was working on his second treatise on architecture, the *Observations sur l'architecture* to be published in 1765, describes it in detail in an important chapter of his new book dealing with the "difficulty of decorating Gothic churches."

During the last years of his life Laugier must have worked extremely hard. As soon as the *Observations* and the last volumes of his Venetian history had been published, he finished a book on the Peace of Belgrade of 1738, begun earlier at Cologne; he worked on a book of art criticism about the appreciation of paintings, the manuscript of which was at the time of his death so far advanced that with a few finishing touches it was published posthumously; he accepted a commission to turn copious material on the history of the troubadours, collected by La Curne de Sainte-Palaye, into a book. He had several other projects in hand: a work dealing with the commerce of the Levant, a continuation of Vertot's history of Malta, a history of the Popes, and an adaptation of Muratori's writings into a general history of Italy. He thus lived the full life of an *homme de lettres* who had achieved recognition and the gratifying reward of academic honors, always in stimulating contact with the great artists and writers of his time. No doubt, Laugier could well be satisfied and feel that the soul-searching and fateful decision to leave the Society of Jesus had been the right one for him.

He died after a short illness on April 5, 1769. His writing desk and the tables of his apartment were full of notes and manuscripts relating to the various projects on which he had been working almost to the end.[16]

Of Laugier's writings it is the *Essai* alone (and to a lesser extent, and only because written by the same author, the *Observations*) which has kept his name alive until today. It was, as already said, well received. But, more than that, it was widely discussed, with two prominent architects and a well-known *homme de lettres* publishing their own criticisms. For a book on architectural theory to have this response was quite extraordinary. There are several reasons for it, one of which was, no doubt, that by the middle of the eighteenth century a wide public had taken a lively interest in art criticism in general and that this new book was felt to belong as much to the art-critical literature as to the long line of treatises on architectural theory.

However, even if written in an elegant style which made the subject matter understandable to the layman, it did deal with architectural theory with which the wider public was not conversant. The professional architects, however, were of course familiar with the subject and knew the relevant literature. In particular those belonging to the older generation believed that the impact the book had undeniably made was undeserved since Laugier's main ideas were already to be found in a book written half a century earlier, the *Nouveau traité de toute l'architecture* by J.L. de Cordemoy, which, his most hostile critic said, Laugier "almost completely copied."[17] The charge that he was more or less reiterating the ideas already set out by Cordemoy has been leveled against Laugier not only in his own time but also in later

[16]The life and work of Laugier are dealt with in greater detail in my "Laugier and Eighteenth Century French Theory," London, A. Zwemmer, 1962.

[17]*Examen d'un Essai sur l'architecture*. Paris, 1753, p. 10. Laugier erroneously believed Frézier to be its author.

years, even quite recently. It is true that a great deal of what Cordemoy says finds an echo in Laugier's book, but it is important to note that Laugier in no way tried to hide this fact. He himself in the preface to the first edition, referred to Cordemoy as the author whom he considered the best of all who had written on architectural theory, whose treatise "contains excellent principles" which, had he developed them further, would have shed a great light on architecture—a task he, Laugier, was going to undertake in his own treatise.[18] This frank admission is unique at a time when eminent authors considered it normal practice to take over whole passages from other writings and never troubled to signify in any way that these passages did not stem from their own pen. Nevertheless, it is true that a number of Laugier's principles can be traced back to Cordemoy—for example the singular quality of the free-standing column, the constructional advantages of coupled columns, the preference of a straight entablature over the usual arcade. Yet, the difference between the two writers is considerable; and it is this difference which reveals another reason why Laugier's book succeeded in "making a stir" while Cordemoy's was almost forgotten until Laugier himself rescued it from oblivion. Where Cordemoy is confused, Laugier is lucid. Where Cordemoy has a vague idea about linking architectural forms to nature, Laugier pronounces the vital principle of the primitive hut, the pivot of all his basic conceptions, a principle at which he arrived quite independently. Laugier is very clear in his mind about what is needed to reform architecture and is therefore able to achieve something never even attempted by Cordemoy—to set out in the preface, the introduction and the first chapter in clear and systematic form a precise program of the architecture to come. He had something to say that needed to be said at that moment.

Therein lies the importance of the book, and this was

[18]See pp. 2 f.

another reason for its immediate success. At the middle of the century rococo had run its course; a longing to return to a simpler, more natural form of art and society was the reaction. Laugier, having a clear conception of at least the principles on which a new style should be founded, set out a program from which, as always happens in this kind of situation, everything that could blur its precision or blunt its decisive diction was excluded. His presumptuous, didactic, overconfident and even arrogant manner, often irritating to the modern reader, was only the outward sign of a deeply felt conviction of the rightness and importance of the message he was going to communicate. It was this decisiveness which appealed to those of his readers who were attuned to the message; it strengthened their belief in a new era to come. His pronouncements that if column, entablature and pediment are "suitably placed and suitably formed, nothing else needs be added to make the work perfect" and that "the parts of an architectural Order are the parts of the building itself" were the mottoes of the neoclassical architecture soon to arise.[19]

This leads to the third reason for the impact the book made and for the notable role it played in the history of art: it was written at exactly the right time. Ten years earlier (though Laugier would hardly have been able to conceive his vision then) the public would not have been ready for it. Ten years later there would have been no need for a prophetic message—neoclassicism had by then arrived.

The two chapters following the first programmatic part are more conventional, dealing in the traditional way with the Orders, with solidity, convenience and *bienséance*. He relies quite frequently on the writings of other authors, but there are also many original observations such as the suggestion to convert the Dome des Invalides into a mausoleum for the kings of France, a suggestion that was taken up—even in

[19]See pp. 13. 153.

details—when, in the next century, the ashes of Napoleon were transferred there.[20]   There is the amusing description of the absurd (and even now unchanged) itinerary to be followed by those wishing to visit the *Galerie des Glaces* in Versailles.[21] There are two further chapters, the fifth and the sixth, one on town planning and the other on garden architecture; they are critical but in no way programmatic. This is not so with the important fourth chapter, headed: "On the Style in Which to Build Churches." Laugier gives in this chapter an application of his principles by describing his plan for a church which, though constructionally impracticable, conveyed the idea of a new style and considerably influenced the younger generation.

Laugier was often quoted during the following decades, in particular by English architects of whom the idiosyncratic Soane appreciated him most. With the advent of Romanticism in the next century his name was almost forgotten. Yet the appeal his book exercised over his contemporaries had still not spent itself; at the beginning of this century no lesser person than Le Corbusier knew Laugier's two books on architecture, quoted him frequently, and took up his story of the creation of the primitive hut in which he too thought to discover a vital principle from which to develop a new style.[22]

Within a few years of the publication of the second edition, the *Essai* was translated into English and German. The text of the English translation, published twice, in 1755 and 1756, under the imprint of two different firms, was even by eighteenth century standards wanting in many respects (a contemporary reviewer called it "wretched"). The present translation is based on the edition of 1753. This was pub-

---

[20]See pp. 92 f.

[21]See pp. 94 f.

[22]I am indebted to Professor Hoesli of Zurich for drawing my attention to LeCorbusier's interest in Laugier's writings.

lished by the firm of Nicolas-Bonaventure Duchesne who received the Royal Privilege on December 22, 1752, after the censor had passed it on November twenty-fifth of the same year with the following remarks: "I have read by Order of Monseigneur the Chancellor a manuscript with the title: *Essai sur l'Architecture,* and have found nothing that would not be in favor of its publication. The author, full of enthusiasm for a celebrated art, tries to contribute to the perfection of this art. The work is very systematic. Furthermore, it is written in an elegant and precise manner, which would make it generally pleasant to read."

The same publisher brought out the second edition of 1755 under the same title but with the following addition: "New edition, revised, corrected and enlarged; with a dictionary of terms and plates which facilitate their explanations. By le P. Laugier of the Society of Jesus." The edition is, indeed, considerably enlarged, mainly by additions in which Laugier gives his reply to criticisms, almost exclusively to those set out in a book entitled *Examen d'un essai sur l'architecture* and published at the end of 1753. Although the author's name did not appear on the title page, it was generally agreed that it was a joint undertaking of the critic LaFont de Saint-Yenne, who was mainly responsible for the preface, and the aged architect Etienne Briseux, who as a professional architect challenged the validity of Laugier's radical statements and queried the soundness of the constructions proposed by him. Laugier's replies are certainly interesting but cannot fail to weaken his categorical assertions by overstating his case and to impair the single-mindedness with which he had developed his theory. It is only in reading the first edition that these qualities are clearly felt. I have incorporated the additions in the translation, leaving them at their proper places within the text, but have marked them in such a way that it should be possible for the reader to disregard them if he wishes to evoke the impression the book made in 1753. On the other hand, he will be able to read without interruption the book in its final form.

Laugier also added an *avertissement* in which he deals too with the *Examen* and which he placed in front of the preface. Although he begins by referring to it in more general terms, he soon goes into the details of two important themes treated in the first edition: his complete rejection of the pilaster and niche and his plan for a church. Since his remarks are only understandable to those who have read the *Essai* itself, I have placed the *avertissement* at the end of the complete text.

London, April 1975   Wolfgang Herrmann.

ESSAI

SUR

L'ARCHITECTURE.

A PARIS,

Chez Duchesne, rue S. Jacques, au
Temple du Goût.

M. DCC. LIII.

Avec Approbation & Privilege du Roy.

Preface

There are several treatises on architecture which explain measures and proportions with reasonable accuracy, enter into the details of the different Orders and furnish models for all manner of buildings. There is no work as yet that firmly establishes the principles of architecture, explains its true spirit and proposes rules for guiding talent and defining taste. It seems to me that in those arts which are not purely mechanical it is not sufficient to know how to work; it is above all important to learn to think. An artist should be able to explain to himself everything he does, and for this he needs firm principles to determine his judgments and justify his choice so that he can tell whether a thing is good or bad, not simply by instinct but by reasoning and as a man experienced in the way of beauty.

Knowledge is far advanced in almost all liberal arts. A great many talented people have applied themselves to make us sensitive to all refinements. They have written with great learning on poetry, painting, and music. The mystery of these ingenious arts has been so thoroughly explored that in this field little is left to be discovered. We have well considered precepts and judicious criticisms which determine their true beauty. Imagination has guidelines which lead it in

1

the right direction and has restraints to curb it. We can accurately assess both the excellence of brilliant traits and the disorder caused by faults. Should there be lack of good poets, painters or musicians, it would not be the fault of theory, but the default of talent.

Only architecture has until now been left to the capricious whim of the artists who have offered precepts indiscriminately. They fixed rules at random, based only on the inspection of ancient buildings. They copied the faults as scrupulously as the beauty; lacking principles which would make them see the difference, they were bound to confound the two. Being servile imitators, they declared as legitimate everything which has been authorized by examples. They always confined their studies to fact and deduced from them, erroneously, the law: thus, their teaching has been nothing but a source of error.

Vitruvius has in effect taught us only what was practiced in his time. Although brilliant flashes herald a genius able to penetrate into the true mystery of his art, he does not make an attempt to tear away the veil which covers it. Always avoiding the depths of theory, he takes us along the road of practice and more than once we go astray. All modern authors, with the exception of M. de Cordemoy, give no more than commentaries on Vitruvius, following him uncritically in all his errors. I say with the exception of M. de Cordemoy, for this author, being more profound than most of the others, saw the truth that was hidden from them. His treatise on architecture is extremely short but contains excellent principles and well-considered notions. If he had developed them further, and drawn from them the right conclusions, he could have shed great light on the obscurity of the art he was writing about and he could have banished the annoying uncertainty that renders rules arbitrary.

Therefore it is to be hoped that some great architect will undertake to save architecture from eccentric opinions by disclosing its fixed and unchangeable laws. All art and all science have a definite objective, but not every road can be equally good to reach it. There is only one that leads directly to that end and it is this unique road which one must know. In all things there is only one way of doing it well. What is art, if not that mode of expression (*manière*) which is based on clear principles and is carried out with the help of unchanging precepts?

Awaiting someone more capable than I am to disentangle the chaotic state of architectural rules, so that from then on there is not a single rule that cannot be clearly explained, I shall try and throw some ray of light on it. Whenever I have looked at our greatest and finest buildings, my soul has been aroused. At times the spell was so strong that it gave rise to pleasure mingled with rapture and enthusiasm. At other times I was not so passionately carried away. I reacted favorably, though to a lesser degree: nevertheless my delight was real. Often I remained entirely indifferent; just as often I was disgusted, shocked and repelled. I have thought a long time about these different reactions. I repeated my observations until I was sure that the same monuments impressed me always in the same way. I sounded the taste of others and, by submitting them to a similar experiment, found that all my own impressions were felt by them more or less vividly according to the different temperament that nature had given them. I then drew these conclusions: (1) that absolute beauty (*beautès essentielles*) is inherent in architecture independent of mental habit and human prejudice; (2) that the composition of a piece of architecture is, like all creative work, susceptible to dullness and liveliness, to propriety and disorder; (3) that there is necessary for this as for any other art talent which cannot be acquired, a measure of inborn genius, and that this talent, this genius, must nevertheless be subject to and governed by laws.

I thought more and more about the diverse impressions

which different architectural works made upon me because I wanted to penetrate to the cause of these effects. I asked myself how to account for my own feelings and wanted to know why one thing delighted me and another only pleased me, why I found one disagreeable, another unbearable. At first, this search led only to obscurity and uncertainty. Yet I was not discouraged; I sounded the abyss until I thought I had discovered the bottom and did not cease to ask my soul until it had given me a satisfying answer. Suddenly a bright light appeared before my eyes. I saw objects distinctly where before I had only caught a glimpse of haze and clouds. I took hold of these objects eagerly and saw by their lights my uncertainties gradually disappear and my difficulties vanish. Finally, I reached the stage where I could, through principles and conclusions, prove to myself the inevitability of these effects without knowing the cause.

This is the road which I followed in order to satisfy myself. It seems to me that it would be useful to let the public know of the success I had had from my efforts. If I could induce my readers to make sure that I have not deceived them, to criticize my conclusions severely and to try themselves to penetrate further into the same abyss, then architecture will have gained infinitely. I can truly say that my main intention is to suggest to the public, especially to the artists, that they should doubt, should make conjectures, and should never be easily satisfied. If, spurred on by me to do their own re-search, they are led to find me wrong, to correct my inac-curacies, and to improve my reasoning, I shall be only too pleased.

This book is just an essay in which I really give no more than indications and clear the way. The task of applying my principles extensively I leave to others who may use a keen intelligence which I would not have. I say enough about this to give architects firm working rules and infallible means to reach perfection. I have tried as much as I could to make myself intelligible. Often I could not avoid using terms of art; nearly all of them are quite well known and there are also dictionaries to explain their true meaning. Since my main purpose is to form the taste of the architects, I leave out those details which can be found elsewhere; nor do I need to burden this little work with drawings which may be irritating and tiring to the reader.[1]

[1]In the second edition the sentence after "elsewhere" is replaced by: "and to make this work more instructive I have added to this second edition a number of plates sufficient to put before the reader all those objects of which a simple description would give him only an imperfect idea."

Introduction

Of all the useful arts, architecture demands the most accomplished talent and the most extensive knowledge. It needs perhaps as much genius, *esprit* and taste to become a great architect as is needed for a first-rate painter or poet. It would be a great mistake to believe that in architecture only mechanics are involved, that it is confined to digging out foundations and raising walls, all according to rules which, becoming a routine, only require eyes accustomed to judge a plumbline and hands fit to handle a trowel.

When one speaks of the art of building, the chaotic mess of clumsy debris, immense piles of shapeless materials, a dreadful noise of hammers, perilous scaffolding, a fearful grinding of machines and an army of dirty and mudcovered workmen—all this comes to the mind of ordinary people, the unpleasant outer cover of an art whose intriguing mysteries, noticed by few people, excite the admiration of all those who penetrate them. There they discover inventions of a boldness that proclaims a great and fertile genius, proportions of a stringency that indicates severe and systematic precision, and ornaments of an elegance that tells of a delicate and exquisite feeling. Whoever is able to grasp true beauty to this extent will, far from confounding architecture with the lesser arts,

7

be inclined to range it among the more profound sciences. The sight of a building, perfect as a work of art, causes a delightful pleasure which is irresistible. It stirs in us noble and moving ideas and that sweet emotion and enchantment which works of art carrying the imprint of a superior mind arouse in us. A beautiful building speaks eloquently for its architect. In his writings M. Perrault is at most a scholar; the Colonnade of the Louvre makes him a great man.

Architecture owes all that is perfect to the Greeks, a nation privileged to have known everything regarding science and to have invented everything connected with the arts. The Romans, able to admire and capable of copying the excellent models which the Greeks had left them, wished to add something of their own and thereby only taught the world that when the stage of perfection is reached there is no other way than to imitate or decline. The barbarism of succeeding centuries, having buried the fine arts under the ruins of the only empire that had preserved taste and principles, called forth a new system of architecture in which neglected proportion and ornament childishly crowded produced nothing but stones in fretwork, shapeless masses and a grotesque extravagance—a new architecture which for too long has been the delight of Europe. Unfortunately, most of our cathedrals are fated to preserve the remains of this style for generations to come. Let us admit, however, that in spite of innumerable faults this architecture had its beauty. Although its most spectacular creations show a coarseness and clumsiness in feeling and spirit that is altogether shocking, we cannot but admire the bold outline, the delicate chiseling and the untrammeled grandeur of some buildings which through these qualities display a kind of inimitable recklessness. But in the end some men of genius, more fortunate, were able to discover in the ancient monuments proof of the universal aberration and the means of reversing the process. Capable of appreciating the marvels which had been on view for so many centuries in vain, they closely observed the proportions and imitated the accomplished workmanship. Through their thorough investigations and experiments they revived the study of sound rules and re-established architecture in all its ancient authority. They gave up the absurd fancy ornaments of the Gothic and Arabesque styles and put in their place the virile and elegant adornment of the Doric, Ionic and the Corinthian. Frenchmen, slow to invent but quick to adopt successful inventions, envied the Italians the glory of having revived the splendid creations of Greece. Many monuments around us are witness to the fact that our forefathers eagerly and successfully competed. We have had our Bramantes, our Michelangelos, our Vignolas. The last century produced masterpieces in architecture worthy of the best ages because at that time nature almost spent itself by lavishing upon us a gift of talent. But at the very moment when we were approaching perfection, as if barbarism had not lost all its claim on us, we fall back into a low and faulty taste. Everything now seems to threaten us with a complete decadence.

This danger, which comes closer every day but can still be averted, prompts me to offer here in all modesty my thoughts on an art that I have always greatly loved. In this I am not motivated by ambition to criticize, an ambition I detest, nor by any desire to say something new, a desire I believe to be at least futile. Full of respect for our artists, many of whom are renowned for their skill, I confine myself to informing them of my ideas and doubts, which I ask them to scrutinize thoroughly. If I decry as an abuse a number of customary features, universally accepted by architects, I do not expect them to accede to my personal opinion which I gladly submit to their intelligent criticism. I only ask them to give up willingly some prejudices which, though common, are yet detrimental to the progress of art.

Do not let it be said that, because I am not a professional

architect, I cannot speak with sufficient knowledge. This, surely, is the least of all difficulties; every time we watch a tragedy, we judge it without ever having written a single word. Nobody is barred from knowing the rules, although to apply them is given only to a few. One should not cite respectable but by no means infallible authorities as evidence against me, since to judge what should be by what is would spoil everything. The greatest men have sometimes gone astray—to take their example always as a rule is therefore not a safe way to avoid errors. No one should try to check me in my course on the pretense of fancied difficulties; idleness finds many, where reason sees none. I am convinced that those of our architects who are genuinely eager to bring their art to perfection will be grateful for my good intentions. They may find in this essay thoughts that had not occurred to them before; if they consider them to be sound, they should not be too proud to make use of them; this is all I ask. [*Therefore to see only with regret that an alien hand carries the torch of truth into mysteries not yet penetrated, to reject out of repugnance to the source from which it comes a light which is offered, to meet with blind contempt an amateur eager to try and find routes leading to the goal missed by other routes, to be passionately against the success which his efforts could attain out of fear of finding thereafter critics more attentive and judges more severe, such a frame of mind is merely that of artists devoid of talent and feeling.*][1]

[1]Passages set in italics and enclosed in brackets are additions made by Laugier for the second edition of 1755.

Chapter I
General Principles of Architecture

It is the same in architecture as in all other arts: its principles are founded on simple nature, and nature's process clearly indicates its rules. Let us look at man in his primitive state without any aid or guidance other than his natural instincts. He is in need of a place to rest. On the banks of a quietly flowing brook he notices a stretch of grass; its fresh greenness is pleasing to his eyes, its tender down invites him; he is drawn there and, stretched out at leisure on this sparkling carpet, he thinks of nothing else but enjoying the gift of nature; he lacks nothing, he does not wish for anything. But soon the scorching heat of the sun forces him to look for shelter. A nearby forest draws him to its cooling shade; he runs to find a refuge in its depth, and there he is content. But suddenly mists are rising, swirling round and growing denser, until thick clouds cover the skies; soon, torrential rain pours down on this delightful forest. The savage, in his leafy shelter, does not know how to protect himself from the uncomfortable damp that penetrates everywhere; he creeps into a nearby cave and, finding it dry, he praises himself for his discovery. But soon the darkness and foul air surrounding him make his stay unbearable again. He leaves and is resolved to make good by his ingenuity the careless neglect of nature. He wants to make himself a dwelling that protects but does not bury him. Some fallen branches in the forest are the right material for his purpose; he chooses four of the strongest, raises them upright and arranges them in a square; across their top he lays four other branches; on these he hoists from two sides yet another row of branches which, inclining towards each other, meet at their highest point. He then covers this kind of roof with leaves so closely packed that neither sun nor rain can penetrate. Thus, man is housed. Admittedly, the cold and heat will make him feel uncomfortable in this house which is open on all sides but soon he will fill in the space between two posts and feel secure.

Such is the course of simple nature; by imitating the natural process, art was born. All the splendors of architecture ever conceived have been modeled on the little rustic hut I have just described. It is by approaching the simplicity of this first model that fundamental mistakes are avoided and true perfection is achieved. The pieces of wood set upright have given us the idea of the column, the pieces placed horizontally on top of them the idea of the entablature, the inclining pieces forming the roof the idea of the pediment. This is what all masters of art have recognized. But take note of this: never has a principle been more fertile in its effect. From now on it is easy to distinguish between the parts which are essential to the composition of an architectural Order and those which have been introduced by necessity or have been added by caprice. The parts that are essential are the cause of beauty, the parts introduced by necessity cause every license, the parts added by caprice cause every fault. This calls for an explanation; I shall try to be as clear as possible.

Let us never lose sight of our little rustic hut. I can only see columns, a ceiling or entablature and a pointed roof forming at both ends what is called a pediment. So far there is no vault, still less an arch, no pedestals, no attic, not even a door or a window. I therefore come to this conclusion: in an architectural Order only the column, the entablature and the pediment may form an essential part of its composition. If each of these parts is suitably placed and suitably formed, nothing else need be added to make the work perfect.

We still have in France a beautiful ancient monument, which in Nimes is called the *Maison Carrée*. Everybody, connoisseur or not, admires its beauty. Why? Because everything here accords with the true principles of architecture: a rectangle where thirty columns support an entablature and a roof—closed at both ends by a pediment—that is all; the combination is of a simplicity and a nobility which strikes everybody. [*The author of the* Examen[1] *disapproves of my intention to establish a strict relation between all parts of our buildings and those of the rustic hut. He should have explained to us in detail the laws which make this relation faulty because if it is based on solid grounds, as I maintain and as all masters of the art have suggested, then no way exists any longer of attacking the rules which I establish in the articles that follow. They are all necessary consequences of this simple principle. If I am to be refuted, the whole line of action amounts to this: either show that the principle is wrong or that the conclusion does not follow from it. One will strike in vain as long as one does not use one or the other of these two weapons against me. All declamations, even all insults will be to no purpose. The judicious reader will always come back to this question: is the principle wrong or the conclusion? The only reason brought up against the proved relation between our buildings and the rustic hut is that we should be allowed to move a little away from this coarse and shapeless invention. We have, indeed, moved far away from it through the grand gout of the decoration which we have put in place of the careless faults of such crude composition, but the essential must remain—the rough sketch which nature offers us. Art must only make use of its resources to*

[1]*Examen d'un essai sur l'architecture*, Paris, 1753. See p. 148. (Translator's note.)

embellish, smoothe and polish the work without touching the substance of the plan.]

Let us now consider in detail the essential parts of an architectural Order.

Article I

The Column

(1) The column must be strictly perpendicular, because, being intended to support the whole load, perfect verticality gives it its greatest strength. (2) The column must be freestanding so that its origin and purpose are expressed in a natural way. (3) The column must be round because nature makes nothing square. (4) The column must be tapered from bottom to top in imitation of nature where this diminution is found in all plants. (5) The column must rest directly on the floor as the posts of the rustic hut rest directly on the ground. All these rules find their justification in our model; all deviations from this model without real necessity must, therefore, be considered as so many faults.

1. Fault: when columns, instead of standing free, are engaged in the wall. The column certainly loses much of its grace when even a small obstacle obscures its outline. I admit that circumstances frequently seem to rule out the use of free-standing columns. People want to live in closed spaces, not in open halls. Therefore, it becomes necessary to fill in the space between the columns and consequently to engage them. In this case, an engaged column will not be regarded as a fault, but as a license sanctioned by necessity. It should, however, always be remembered that any license points to an imperfection and must be used cautiously and only when it is impossible to find a better way. If, therefore, the columns have to be engaged, the degree of engagement should be as small as possible—a quarter at most or even less so that, even

when constrained, they retain some quality of the freedom and ease which gives them so much grace. We must avoid getting into the awkward situation where engaged columns have to be employed. It would be best to reserve the use of columns for peristyles where they can be completely free-standing and to omit them altogether whenever necessity compels us to back them onto a wall. After all, even though we have to submit to *bienséance* why should we not disengage the column so that it can be seen in the round? Would the facade of St. Gervais not be improved if the Doric columns were free-standing like those of the upper Orders? Is there anything impossible in this? [*The architect, who to justify this fault shelters behind the argument that the part of the architrave over the center door looked too weak to carry the entablature and the crowning pediment, does not notice that instead of preventing one irregularity he sets up two which are considerably worse. What necessity is there for a complete entablature if its weight cannot be carried by the architrave? Will he even have us maintain that the first pediment is within the rules? Had the columns of the first Order been free-standing, the upper Orders would have had nonetheless all the necessary diminution because of their smaller module and greater lightness.*]

To dare criticize a work which the public commonly takes for a faultless masterpiece suggests that one defers little to public opinion. However, pointing out the defects of this building gives me the right to be unsparing in my criticism of any other building without hurting anybody's pride. That is why I shall speak bluntly. After what I have said, it will be less surprising that the connoisseurs set so little value on the Church of the Jesuits in the rue St. Antoine. Without counting other faults, of which there are many, the effect of the three Orders of engaged columns is most disagreeable. This, as M. de Cordemoy so adroitly says, is no more than architecture in relief to which the eyes of enlightened people will never be reconciled. I have often bemoaned the craze of architects for engaged columns, but I should never have believed that it could occur to the mind of a thinking person to engage one column into the other. No fault is more unbearable, more shocking than this. Even those new to architecture will agree on this, and yet this fault is repeatedly committed on all four sides of the inner courtyard of the Louvre. Such a glaring blunder on such a magnificent work of art ranks among the degradations of the human spirit.

2. Fault: when instead of round columns pilasters are used. Pilasters are only a poor representation of columns. Their corners indicate a constraint of art and deviate noticeably from the simplicity of nature; their sharp and awkward edges hurt the eye, their surfaces, not being rounded, make the whole Order seem flat. They are not adaptable to that diminution which makes columns so attractive. Pilasters are never necessary; wherever they are used, columns could be applied just as advantageously. They must, therefore, be regarded as a bizarre innovation, in no way founded on nature or authorized by any need, which can only have been adopted out of ignorance and is still tolerated only by habit. The fashion for pilasters has triumphed everywhere: alas, where are they not to be found? Yet to realize how distasteful they are, one only needs to think of the grand effect which columns always make, an effect that is unfailingly destroyed by pilasters. Change the coupled columns of the Colonnade of the Louvre into pilasters and you take away all its beauty. Compare the two wings of this superb facade with the pavilions at both corners: what a difference! Even valets and maidservants want to know why the pavilions are different from the rest. This vexation is aroused by the taste for true beauty, a taste that is natural to everybody. The identical architectural Order extends over the whole facade, but the main part has columns, the pavilions have pilasters; this difference alone is enough to disturb the pleasure that a more

unified whole would have given. [*It is of no avail to say that diversity, so precious in art, demands variation in the decoration of the pavilions. No doubt one must, if possible, make variations, but without departing from the laws of nature. Otherwise who will prevent an artist, intent on even more variation, from replacing round columns with oval ones or prism-shaped ones or with pillars having five, six or eight faces? By which principles would it be possible to forbid him these extravagances* (bizzarreries)? *It is even less reasonable to plead in excuse the impossibility of harmoniously linking the facade of the porticoes with the one facing the river. The pilasters on the second facade need only be suppressed to visualize one of better taste.*]

On entering the nave of the Chapel of Versailles everybody is struck by the beauty of its columns, by the picturesque vista (*âpreté*) through its intercolumniations; but as soon as one approaches the apse, there is not a person who does not notice with regret the stupid interruption of the beautiful row of columns by a depressing pilaster. One can, therefore, be quite certain that the use of pilasters is one of the great abuses that have found their way into architecture, and since an abuse never comes alone we have been presented with folded pilasters in corners, with curved pilasters in circular buildings, with pilasters lost in the confused interpenetration of one into the other. The pilaster is a frivolous ornament which has been put to all sorts of uses; it has even been married to a column which, it seems, is there as its inseparable companion. Has there ever been a more ridiculous match? What does the engaged column mean behind a free-standing column? Honestly, I do not know and I defy anybody to explain it. Does it make sense to unite two things which are quite incompatible? The column has its diminution, whereas the pilaster could not have any which is the reason that the latter will always look either too narrow at the bottom or too wide at the top. Whenever there is a void to be filled, one fills it

17

with a pilaster; whenever there is a fault to be covered up or a place to be embellished, one cuts out one half or one quarter of a pilaster. The ancients were not more scrupulous about this matter, at times even less particular, than the moderns, since they built colonnades where they mixed columns and pilasters. In short, the pilaster is a thing I cannot bear. This is an inborn aversion. The more I studied architecture, the more I found in its true principles the justification for my own aversion. [*Besides, while on the subject, it is not at all my personal taste which I set up as rule; it would be quite unfair to allege that I only condemn pilasters because of my blind aversion. The reasons I gave for it prove that my hatred is well founded.*]

It will be said that pilasters are used so as to avoid the excessive cost of columns. To that I answer: if the column is barred only for reasons of economy, all that is needed is a decision to suppress architectural Orders altogether. Beautiful buildings can be created without their help, but if one wants to employ the five Orders I shall never forgive cutting out the column which is their most essential part.

3. Fault: to give a swelling to the shaft at about the third of its height instead of tapering the column in the normal way. I do not believe that nature has ever produced anything that could justify this swelling. Let us do justice to our artists who a long time ago have given up spindle-shaped columns which are not to be found on any recent work. Rusticated columns are no less faulty than spindle-shaped columns. Philibert de l'Orme had a high opinion of rusticated columns and covered the Palais des Tuileries with them. His taste, however, was not sufficiently refined to make them admissible on his authority alone. This great man deserves to be highly praised and will always be counted among the great masters of architecture. We owe to him the rebirth of this beautiful art in our country, yet his work still savors of the depraved taste of the preceding centuries. Rusticated columns

are only a capricious fancy; we do not see a whole column but various drums of a different scale piled up one above the other, producing an effect which is rather mean and infinitely harsh. The beautiful Palais de Luxembourg is quite disfigured by these rusticated columns. Far worse are spiral columns. Whoever thought of them was certainly skillful because it needs much skill to make them well; but had he had judicious taste, he would surely not have taken so much care in carrying out such a foolish invention. Spiral columns are to architecture what the bandy legs of a cripple are to the human body; yet at first their peculiar appearance pleased some people who were enemies of the natural and who believed the work to be beautiful because it was difficult. Others, more eccentric still, have offered us stumps of straight columns on which they had mounted in a most miserable manner two-thirds of a spiral column; others again, prompted by the same taste but defeated by practical difficulties, wanted at least the satisfaction of twisting the flutings of straight columns. These absurdities have been reserved mainly for altars. I admire the baldachins of St. Peter's in Rome, of the Val de Grâce and of the Invalides, but I shall never forgive the great men who designed them for using twisted columns. Do not let us be deceived by false jewels: they only demonstrate the failings of a genius. Let us keep to the simple and natural; it is the only road to beauty. [*Against this it is said that in light and elegant constructions which do not demand great solidity spiral columns, far from hurting the eyes, "will always give pleasure" and be willingly accepted. The reason on which this opinion is based is that of diversity. But, once more, does the wish for diversity authorize every kind of fancy? Would columns fluted in twisting spirals be proper for a light and elegant construction even though solidity would not be affected? Undoubtedly not, because they would be contrary to nature. Therefore, one must always come back to nature to forestall flights of fancy and must not believe one has given unanswerable proof of it when saying: "This is accepted practice, therefore it is good; this is irregular but has gained the right to please, therefore one must be very careful about banning it." One day, somebody said to me: "Monsieur, why do you condemn things which please me?" I answered: "For the same reason, Monsieur, that you condemn the farces of the charlatans which please many people."]*

4. Fault: when the columns, instead of resting directly on the ground, are raised on pedestals. Since the columns are, if I may say so, the legs of a building, it is absurd to give them another pair of legs. The pedestals I am speaking of have been invented out of misfortune. If columns were found to be too short, it was decided to put them on stilts in order to make up for the lack of height. The same difficulty led to having recourse to double pedestals when a single pedestal was not sufficient. Nothing makes a building look more heavy and clumsy than these huge angular masses which serve as substructures to the columns. The colonnade of the Hôtel Soubise is unbearable because of these hideous pedestals; but if the columns were rising from the ground, it would be a charming building. Columns may rest on a massive, continuous wall, that is to say on a simple socle without base, without cornice and of medium height; and this will be done whenever a colonnade is being built and the level of the inner floor is higher than the surrounding ground. Far from criticizing this practice, I am convinced that it will always be successful. Sometimes too, when the intercolumniations are filled by a balustrade as at the bay of the Chapel of Versailles and of the Colonnade of the Louvre, each column may rest separately on a small socle. This second manner is less perfect and would even be defective if it were not justified by the necessity of having a balustrade on a colonnade which is erected on the first floor; but to place pedestals under columns at ground level is an inexcusable fault. Nearly all the

altars in our churches present this ridiculous sight. Columns are needed here but they would cost too much if they were on a scale large enough to make them rest directly on the floor—hence one needs pedestals. This is the reason why the columns at the main altar of the Church of the Jesuits in the rue St. Antoine are set on two pedestals, one above the other. Only this once shall I cite this shocking work. All one can say about it is that none of the glaring blunders that architects can make has been forgotten here. [*Objections are raised against the ridiculous effect of columns placed on the floor as part of the altar table. Never, I reply, has it been my intention to make use of sham columns with which one decorates retables. If, however, one insists on such a decoration, I think that a demi-dome where columns, placed on the floor, have their entablature surmounted by a demi-cupola with the altar standing free in the center would be preferable to all those columns on stilts which make the altar table look like a miserable stylobate.*] In short, pedestals are only good for carrying statues and to make them serve any other purpose is essentially bad taste. However much it is said that pedestals have been admitted at all times, that Vitruvius and all his commentators assign to each Order its particular pedestal and that they are to be found on the most beautiful buildings of antiquity, I have my principle which I shall never give up. Any device—even if approved by great men—which is either contrary to nature or cannot be convincingly explained is a bad device and must be proscribed.

[*The author of the* Examen *opposes this principle by saying that we should not approach nature too closely and lose the opportunity of making our enjoyment more lively through the fortunate effect of an* approved *irregularity. "Let us not,"* he says, *"be slaves to primitive practices; let us not demand too strict a correlation with them in our formations when the* length of time and the force of an ancient habit have authorized these." *This means that irregularities can in time become legitimate, and that whereas the ancients had the right to condemn certain abuses while they were novel, we are not allowed to proscribe them, since they have been sanctioned by the length of time and the force of habit. This way of thinking which makes what is right simply dependent on custom seems to me a very easy expedience for ignorant and lazy artists but it obstructs the progress of the arts too much to be generally adopted. I have always believed that what is originally an abuse does not cease to be one by having become customary. In matters of reason and taste, what has once been condemned should always be condemned. In this sphere good and bad produce two indelible qualities the essence of which neither length of time nor prolonged habit can change or destroy. If only arbitrary rules are wanted for the arts one can insist on custom, but if the processes of art must go back to fixed principles it is necessary to appeal to reason against custom and to sacrifice to the light of one the force and sway of the other.*]

Article II

The Entablature

The entablature is the second part which appears in the model of the rustic hut. The pieces of wood which rest horizontally on the vertical posts to form a ceiling are represented by what we call the entablature. Adhering to our model we come to these conclusions: (1) that the entablature must always rest on its columns like a lintel (*en plate-bande*); (2) that in its whole length it must not have any corner or projection. From there follows condemnation of the following faults:

1. Fault: instead of giving the entablature the form of a true beam carried solely by free-standing columns, to support it by wide arches, a far too common practice in our churches

and elsewhere. Arches are faulty: (1) Because they require massive piers and imposts which, backed against columns, take away the air of lightness (*dégagement*) which is the main beauty of columns and make the whole structure look heavy. (2) Because with these piers we are back to pilasters and their drawbacks. Piers present us with squares, angles and corners, that is, with forms which stray from the natural and savor of constraint; their appearance could not have the unspoiled grace of exquisitely rounded columns. (3) Because arches are used here for a purpose contrary to nature. Arches are vaults. Vaults must always be carried and can never serve as supports. Now, here, they serve no other purpose than to carry the entablature, for if this is not their function of what use can they be? (4) Because arches by their thrust force the columns to give lateral support which, again, is against nature, since columns are made to give vertical support only. Therefore, arches are undoubtedly defective.

I go further: arches are entirely useless. An entablature extended *en plate-bande* over columns does not need arches for support. I know that when a lintel is to bridge an excessively large span, it will not stay up because its supports are too wide apart. But what need is there to make architraves span distances so great that the sight would be frightening? Why be sparing with columns when a judicious increase in numbers will always give singular pleasure? Architects know how far one can extend the width of intercolumniations without reducing in any way the solidity of a building. The ancients have left us infallible rules on the subject; the moderns have discovered the secret which allows more room to move: they thought of coupling columns, a delightful idea which had never occurred to the ancients. Why wish to go beyond it at the risk of replacing delicate elegance by massive heaviness? If it is still maintained that straight architraves (*en plates-bandes*) are incompatible with solidity, then I refer to the evidence of the peristyle of the

Louvre and the Chapel of Versailles, two examples that are remarkable for giving conclusive proof to the contrary. One does not need to be a connoisseur to admire these two beautiful buildings which are bold and yet refined, delicate and yet solid. Their beauty strikes everybody because it is natural, because it is true. It is surprising that, with these models under their eyes, our architects always come back to their miserable arcades.

[*It seems that they are determined to stick to them; we are warned that they have all revolted against a system which tends to suggest the uselessness of arcades. A person who pretends to be their protector and does not always merit the title declares flatly that they are all convinced that arcades make a better effect than straight entablatures. I do not believe at all that this is their opinion but think that those who are really enlightened bear with the arcades only because they believe them to be necessary for the sake of solidity. This, however, is precisely what should be examined patiently and in good faith. Nothing could be more important than to find means by which to avoid the annoying need of using, instead of columns, thick piers with arcades which are really arches of a bridge. Whatever the author of the* Examen *says about it, such means are in no way impossible; and I should not think much of his skill if his great experience does not make him find any.*]

2. Fault: when the line of the entablature is not straight but is broken by angles and projections. The entablature represents the long piece of wood meant to carry the roofing. Would anybody ever have the idea, an extremely ridiculous one, of making this piece out of projections and recesses? How unnecessary! How bizarre! I say the same of those entablatures that are made to jut out over the columns and to recede over the intercolumniations. This mass of protruding and receding angles certainly makes it more difficult of execution, but presents only a medley without taste or design.

These irregularities on a continuous entablature are only excusable at the juncture of a pavilion where it is sensible to have an interruption. But the general use of pavilions is, if I am not mistaken, nothing less than arbitrary. The only legitimate pavilions I know are distributed over a length of a facade like so many small buildings separate from the main body; all the others are purely capricious. [*It is said that this reasoning has not yet entered the mind of any architect. If this is so, then I am sorry, but it does not at all prove that the reasoning is bad.*]

Because it has been noticed that the pavilions I have just mentioned look well on a large building, it has been believed that one could indulge one's fancy in pavilions without restraint. In the hands of mediocre architects the pavilion has become an ornament, an expedient for all occasions, whenever they wished to avoid monotony. This is an abuse. I always come back to my main principle: never to put anything into a building for which one cannot give a sound reason. The idea held by many people that in matters of taste there is no need for the application of a severe rational test is the most fatal of all prejudices.

Article III

The Pediment

The last part of the building is the pediment. It represents the gable of the roof and, therefore, can never be anywhere except across the width of a building. Its inherent shape is triangular and its place must always be above the entablature. The conclusion to be drawn from all this is to reject the following faults.

1. Fault: to erect the pediment on the long side of a building. Since the pediment represents the gable of a roof, it must be placed so as to conform to the thing it represents; the

gable, however, is always set across the width and never along the length of a building. If only our architects would think a little about this reasoning, which is simplicity itself, it would not occur to them to place in the center of a long facade sham pediments which do not signify anything. They believe the facade is made more attractive by thus interrupting uniformity but they should know that in all the arts it is a sin against the rules to use superfluous things. [*It is pointless to argue about the difficulty of reconciling the height of the pediment prescribed by good rule with the height which roofs need in a climate as rainy as ours. An ordinary stonemason would not be checked by this alleged difficulty. There is no need to apply pediments; but if one wants to make use of them it is necessary, and even quite easy, to place them along the width of the building.*] I always notice with regret that the great man who made the design for the peristyle of the Louvre was so thoughtless as to erect a large pediment in the middle. This pediment is even more misplaced than the balustrade which, extending all along the top of the entablature, necessarily indicates a building covered by a flat roof so that anything suggesting the idea of a pointed roof becomes extremely shocking here. [*Yet, the author of the* Examen *undertakes to justify this pediment. Not content to declare it legitimate he asserts that according to my principles it is absolutely necessary. This is a very peculiar logic which I honestly confess I do not understand at all. The pediment in question is reprehensible because the roof is omitted over the whole length of the facade as is proved by the balustrade.*] Even more awkward is the fact that the pediment cuts into the balustrade, a miserable way of joining them. At least we have been spared the horrible fault which some architects have committed, namely to make their balustrade climb up the inclines of the pediment. What shall I say of that long line of pediments which crown the great gallery of the Louvre? What a dull imitation of roofs in the German style!

Almost the only pediments which, in my view, are admissible are those that cover the facade of a church. There they are at their right place. Everywhere else they are usually misplaced since high-pitched roofs are not the fashion anymore.

2. Fault: to make pediments that are not triangular. The roof always ends in a more or less acute angle, and the pediment which is its representation must strictly imitate this shape. Accordingly, curved pediments are unnatural; all the more detestable are broken pediments because they presuppose a half-open roof, while for even stronger reasons scrolled pediments are of all follies the most consummate ones.

3. Fault: to pile pediments on top of each other. Nothing is more absurd than this practice. The pediment below implies a roof, the pediment above again implies a roof; so there are two roofs one over the other. The facade of St. Gervais has this fault, which greatly detracts from its merit. However strong the bias of this building, I do not believe, after the reasons I have given, that any sensible person could approve of a double pediment, one at the top, the other at the bottom. It is even worse when the pediment is placed under the entablature. Using it in this way is like putting the roof inside the house and the ceiling over the roof. Yet how many examples of it exist! How many doors, how many windows are surmounted by a ridiculous pediment!

Article IV

The Different Stories of a Building

Sometimes it is necessary to place several architectural Orders one above the other, either because the building under construction must have several stories or because, even with one floor only, *bienséance* or some other motif demands an elevation for which a single architectural Order is insufficient. In such a case, Orders one above the other become a license, authorized by necessity, and will in no way be reprehensible provided the following rules are observed.

1. Everything which represents the idea of a roof must be eliminated from the lower Orders because to build on top of the roof would be absurd. Consequently, pediments should above all disappear as well as modillions, dentils, triglyphs and mutules which in the opinion of all masters of art represent the terminal sections of different pieces of carpentry. To admit them here is an offense against good rules and a blunder the more glaring since there is no compulsion to commit it. I go further and say that one must also eliminate from the lower Order the whole portion of the entablature which is called frieze and cornice so as to leave only a simple architrave. The reason is this: the great projection of cornices was only invented to serve as support for the overhanging roofs which are there to keep the downpour of water away from the walls. Therefore, it is certain that any cornice recalls the idea of a roof and, consequently, it should have its place only at the uppermost story. Besides, the great projection of cornices interrupts too abruptly, disturbs harmony and presents only separate parts which together do not result in a whole. The column and the whole entablature make a complete building. Therefore, giving each story a whole entablature is like placing several buildings on top of each other. If, on the other hand, each story has just a simple architrave, the complete entablature is reserved for the uppermost story; then there will be coherence and unity and the different parts will really compose a whole. The projection of the cornice is in itself very inconvenient. Rainwater stays on top and in time works havoc. Consequently the cornice becomes heavy so that the construction must be essentially massive or it will without fail fall in ruins. The new facade of St. Sulpice proves only too clearly the truth of my statement. The Doric entablature over the first Order with its enormous projection of the cornice is exposed to all the

inconveniences I have just mentioned. The two towers with complete entablatures on each floor do not resemble towers at all; the two cornices interrupt, separate, and disfigure the whole. Thus, even though practice to the contrary is almost universal, it would be desirable whenever Order is placed above Order to terminate the lower Orders by a simple architrave which, representing a ceiling, quite naturally marks the divisions of the stories. At most, it would be permissible to add to it some parts of the cornice such as an ovolo, a fillet, and a cyma in order to increase the distance between the bases of the upper and the capitals of the lower columns. [*The Critic asks what the effect would be of a simple architrave over a facade as long as the Tuileries, especially if the same Order had been used on the extension to the palace as on the center part. To this I reply that raising such difficulties always surprises me when coming from an architect. If I were consulted about the decoration of a facade as long as that of the Tuileries, I would mainly recommend two things: first, to treat the architectural composition on a grand scale and, second, to vary it considerably and take great care not to let the same member, whatever it may be, run from one end to the other. I would want advancing pavilions, with some parts higher and some lower, with great unity and still greater variety. In this way, I would succeed in avoiding all faults which, it is said, are inevitable in my system and would prove to the Critic who is willing to grant me the talent of writing well that, whatever he says, I understand what I write.*]

2. Care should always be taken to place the heavier Order below the lighter one. Nature dictates this rule and, in general, practice conforms to it. In this way one can, if necessary, make compositions of two, three, four, or even five Orders. But when finally the last Order has been reached which alone should have its complete entablature, I cannot see what significance the usual addition of a superfluous

half-story, called attic, could have. No other part has proportions more irregular and more faulty than this attic story. It gives the rather mean image of a few dormer windows cut into the roof, since there is only the roof above the cornice. The attic story can therefore only spoil the whole building by crowning it in a way that is piteously wretched. The great garden front of the Chateau de Versailles is irritating because of this miserable attic which runs along its top from one end to the other. The attic only needs to be taken away and the balustrade to be placed directly above the cornice to satisfy eye and taste. Should it be said that without an attic story a facade of such length would not have had sufficient height, my answer is that a second Order only needed to be added over the first and all the necessary height would have been there.

3. Whenever there are several stories to a building, it needs as many Orders as there are stories, because if a single Order comprises several stories, they will in effect be only mezzanines, a miserable state of affairs. The architrave alone conveys the idea of a ceiling, therefore each ceiling needs a new architrave and consequently a new Order. This rule has been exactly followed in the facades of the inner courtyards of the Louvre and of the old palace of the Tuileries, but it is ridiculous to have departed from it in the pavilions added to the old palace and in the building which, on the side facing the river, forms the great gallery. It is strange that, wishing to lengthen the facade of the Tuileries by means of the pavilions, preference has been given to an architectural system which has no relation to that of the old building. It only needed some common sense to avoid such a peculiar and shocking contrast. There have been architects, not satisfied with extending one and the same Order over two stories, who carried foolishness to the point where they placed the small Order below a greater one which is like building one house inside another. The facade of St. Peter's in Rome provides an

example of this bad taste; it is found again at the great choir screen of St. Sulpice and at many other places.

4. When placing two Orders one above the other, one must avoid the *porte-à-faux* which of all defects is the most contrary to nature. It is, therefore, necessary that the axes of the upper and lower columns correspond vertically, forming only one perpendicular line. Sometimes there is a large column at the ground floor carrying two smaller ones. This is one of the most glaring faults; the number of columns of the upper Order must be neither more nor less than that of the lower Order. Here I am forced to raise my voice against domes with which so many people seem to be in love. However much is said in their favor, it will still always be true that it is a dreadful thing to see a whole peristyle of columns supported by four great arches which provide it with a foundation that is unsound because it is hollowed out. [*It is a very poor expedient to replace the columns here with pilasters. The* porte-à-faux *is not at all changed through this disagreeable substitution; a tower built over the outer surface of a vault is always extremely shocking.*] All architects agree that void should be over void and solid over solid. Yet drums of domes with an architectural Order always place the solid over the void. If domes are to be built, they should be made differently from the present manner. An architect would give proof of his genius if he invented a way of constructing domes which, while avoiding the intolerable *porte-à-faux*, still retain their attraction. If that is not possible, it is much better not to build them at all. I must also point out that, if domes are built, the roof must not appear at all on the outside, because it is extremely ridiculous to show a tower built over the framework of a roof. In this respect, not to mention a thousand other faults, the Church of the Jesuits in the rue St. Antoine sins in a most atrocious manner. [*That of the Invalides is not so disagreeable because no part of the roof is seen around it. The outside of this dome, and also that of St.*

Peter's in Rome, is a very satisfactory sight because it seems to rest on the foundation. It is not the same inside; in both churches the porte-à-faux *is very noticeable. In reply to this it is said that one does not wish to change a custom with which one is well satisfied. That is all right, but if one imagines to prove thereby that my system is in every respect defective, one is mistaken.*]

Speaking of *porte-à-faux* I should not forget to condemn those pieces of architecture that rest on nothing. Such are fancy columns held up by consoles, arches which are not supported by a pier and other similar daring feats which only dazzle fools. I was one day shown a rood screen in a church set on top of three arches which were held precariously in midair by supports in the form of corbels. I was told: "Look, there is a pretty daring piece." "This is true," I replied, "but if your architect had made this screen with a plain lintel in place of these frightful corbels, his work, without being less daring, would have been more natural; it would have had fewer admirers, but they would have been more distinguished." In short, everything that goes against nature may be peculiar but will never be beautiful. Every part of a building must be supported from the foundation upward. Here is a rule from which it is never permitted to depart.

Article V
Windows and Doors

A building of free-standing columns carrying an entablature needs no doors or windows; but, being open on all sides, it is uninhabitable. The need for protection from the inclemencies of the weather and other more engaging motives force us to fill in the intercolumniations and, consequently, doors and windows are needed. Their shapes are determined by what is convenient; it would be well also to make them elegant. The square is the simplest and the most convenient shape because the leaves of doors and windows open with perfect ease and do not need molded recesses (*arrière-voussures*), the work of which savors of art and constraint, nor do they need casings which also are hardly natural. It is thought that curving the top of doors and windows gives them more grace. But what happens? This curve leaves irregular shapes on either side of the wall, that is a right-angled triangle of which two sides are straight and the hypotenuse is curved. Irregular spaces of this kind always look bad in architecture; they are bound to be filled with bizarre ornaments which are placed there for no other reason than to cover up a fault. It would be much better to avoid this. Semicircular openings must be reserved for triumphal arches where custom has sanctioned them. Everywhere else they are out of tune. Nowadays there is a craze for semicircular windows, but I doubt that one could find examples among the good monuments of antiquity. Still, they are more acceptable than windowheads of an extremely flattened segmental arch. Windows of this kind, which are very common today, have nearly all the inconvenience of semicircular windows and stray even further from nature because of the extreme irregularity of their shape. [*The author of the* Examen *stands firmly by the use of arched windows and highly praises molded recesses. I am far from belittling the usefulness of such a beautiful invention; its stonecutting is subtle and clever; yet is it necessary to make use of this science here? When molded recesses are absolutely necessary the practice is very good, but to use them repeatedly without necessity means pedantically flaunting one's knowledge; this display is characteristic only of those who have no great knowledge. Rectangular windows are more natural than arched windows; it would be in vain to argue with me about that. The idea of covering the irregular spaces left on both sides of arched windows by figures resting on the archivolts—proposed by the Critic and only too often*

33

executed—confirms the need to proscribe this type of window. It is an abuse which leads to a still greater abuse.]

Windows must always be underneath the entablature. If placed above the cornice, they are just dormers. It is deplorable to find in almost all our modern churches no windows other than dormers cutting into the vault.

Windows in a row must always have the same shape; I cannot see the basis for the eccentricity of some architects who have made it their business to vary them.

Because windows and doors only incidentally enter into the composition of an architectural Order, they must never encroach on the essential parts. Whoever mutilated the architrave of the large side pavilions of the Tuileries in order to increase the height of the windows did not know his profession. Unfortunately, M. Perrault, once more unthinkingly, placed at the foot of his superb peristyle of the Louvre a great semicircular arch which cuts into the upper socle on which the columns stand.

So far I have reviewed all the necessary parts of an Order without meeting a niche on my way. What in effect is a niche? What is its use? Honestly, I do not know at all. I do not believe that common sense could put up with the sight of a statue placed in a window which is cut into a curved recess (*en tour creuse*). My aversion to niches is unshakeable, and until I have been shown their need and principle, I shall make a clean sweep of all niches which show up. The only unaffected and elegant place for a statue is on a pedestal. Why cram it into the hollow of a wall and thereby efface its outlines? [*At this point, the author of the* Examen *bursts out into most amusing exclamations. He asks me where I might have traveled not to have met a niche on my way. How could he have been misled by this phrase? Does he imagine that I have not seen any kind of niches which have been so lavishly used on buildings? Yes, indeed, this is how he interprets my thought, and he believes he understands me. At the same time, so as to confound me he cites a vast number of examples and asks where my eyes are. I guarantee him that I keep them wide open. The way on which I have not met niches is the one I have traveled when proceeding from principles to conclusions. I have read and reread all he says in favor of niches and still do not know on what their use may reasonably be founded.*]

I should like to have explained to me the significance of the great volutes which commonly flank the upper part of the facades of our churches. [*In vain, to justify them, are they called* adoucissements *designed to join in an agreeable way the lower to the upper story.*] These volutes can only represent buttresses or flying buttresses, a disagreeable feature which savors too much of toil and labor to be exposed to the eye. Where buttresses are absolutely necessary, architecture would be rendered an outstanding service if they could be effaced.

I feel how perilous it is to denounce common practices. Our artists might well hate me for having disturbed them in their present enjoyment of indulging in liberties which I condemn. But I beg them not to sacrifice those principles, on which the true perfection of their art depends, to notions derived from prejudice or indolence. It will be, no doubt, hard for them to admit that they were mistaken; but if one is in a position, as they are, to do things correctly, such admission, with pride humbled a little, will serve to encourage emulation. The question here is not at all of complying slavishly with custom or of blindly following a routine but of examining whether my ideas are right, whether they have a definite connection (*liaison nécessaire*) with principles accepted by everybody. These principles I have stated truthfully. I have tried to draw the logical conclusions and have established them as rules. I have not excluded exceptions which real necessity authorizes. I have admitted them as permissible licenses provided they are used in a sober and judicious manner. I have boldly dealt with faults, that is, with everything which has no connection with the principles or is not authorized by need. This is my method. If it is bad and can be proved to be so, I shall make it my duty to amend it.

I shall be told: "It therefore follows that our greatest architects committed the most glaring blunders, that each of them departed as a matter of course from your severe rules and, if we are to believe you, that everything admired by us as a masterpiece would be full of faults." I admit that this is a strong objection. Nobody feels less inclined to sully the reputation of the masters of the art than I do. I value their talent, I respect their memory, and my reverence for them is most sincere. But, after all, it would be blind prejudice to believe that everything they have done is good just because they have done it. By supposing that they could have committed faults and that in fact they have committed them, I only recognize that they were men. If the severity of the rules, which I have just set forth, gives occasion to criticize their best works, what will be the consequence? We shall advance beyond them, art will become more perfect, the beauty of their works will be imitated, their faults be avoided. Rules which make this discerning judgment easy are too useful to be discarded.

Another objection will perhaps be made, namely that I reduce architecture to almost nothing, since with the exception of columns, entablatures, pediments, doors, and windows I more or less cut out the rest. It is true that I take away from architecture much that is superfluous, that I strip it of a lot of trash of which its ornamentation commonly consists and only leave it its natural simplicity. But let there be no mistake about it: I do not take away anything from the work or the resources of the architect. I force him always to proceed in a simple and natural manner and never to present anything that savors of art and constraint. Those belonging to the profession will agree that, far from reducing their work, I sentence them to take great pains and to work with an extraordinary degree of precision. Moreover, I leave to the architect ample resources. If he is gifted and has a slight knowledge of geometry he will, with what little I place in his hands, find the secret of varying his plans ad infinitum and of regaining through the diversity of forms what he loses on superfluous parts which I have taken away from him. For many centuries we have combined, always in a different manner, the seven tones of the musical scale and are still far from having exhausted all possible combinations. I say the same of those parts that are the essential elements of an architectural Order. They are small in number yet, without adding anything, one can combine them ad infinitum. It is a sign of genius to know how to avail oneself of these different combinations, this source of pleasing variety. An architect adheres to irrelevancies only because he lacks genius; he overloads his work only because he is not gifted enough to make it simple.

Finally, the objection may be made that a number of my rules, though admirable in theory, become impossible in practice, that for instance columns alone are too weak to support a building and that architraves *en plate-bande* lack solidity. I have already cited examples which completely demolish this objection. What has been done can well be done again. Anyone who studies the peristyle of the Louvre and the bays of the Chapel of Versailles will see the impossibility disappear. Besides, what are the reasons for maintaining that columns are too weak a support? Have they less strength than pilasters? Is strength linked rather to the square than to the round? The proportions of columns are determined by the principles of solidity. As long as columns are strictly vertical, they will without effort carry everything they should carry. Why maintain that straight entablatures threaten to collapse? They will indeed if the size of the intercolumniations is greater than the rules allow; they will, if again contrary to rules, the weight of the massive wall bears upon them. If, however, the intercolumniations are well spaced, if above the architraves is only placed what should be there, namely the frieze and cornice and at most a light balustrade, then there is nothing ever to be afraid of. It is the wall that causes all superfluous weight, it is the wall again that deprives architecture of all its grace. The less it appears, the more beautiful the building will be; and when it does not appear at all, that building will be perfect. [*The Critic who has taken upon himself the task of proving to everybody that the content of this chapter is only a tissue of errors, false reasonings, palpable absurdities, a schoolboy's blunders, denounces here, with his usual moderation, the blind arrogance which has made me fear the consequences of the frankness with which I condemn the customs dear to our artists. He tells me politely in their name that my work, deserving only their contempt, has brought upon me only their indifference. His language would have proved to me the opposite were it not for such an explicit and definite declaration. He repeats a hundred and one times that my ideas will not make any change in the established practice, that I should be ashamed about my disgraceful aberrations and should learn to be wiser and more modest. I have never claimed that my opinion alone should be the law to architects nor have I ever hoped that there would be many among them capable of restricting themselves to the method I propose to them. But I ask them for my part not to demand blind acquiescence in their decisions. That they have the freedom to act as they always have been used to do if the public is satisfied, to that I consent with all my heart. But they have no right to forbid us freedom of thought or even to speak abusively of those who are not so complaisant as to believe that only architects are allowed to talk about architecture. The arts can be under real obligation to persons other than artists; everybody is entitled to propose systems for the perfection of the arts.*]

Chapter II
The Different Architectural Orders

The number of architectural Orders is not definitely fixed. The Greeks knew only three. The Romans counted five and we Frenchmen would like to add a sixth Order. As this is a matter of taste and talent, it seems natural to let artists have complete freedom in this respect. We are not in a worse position than the Greeks and Romans. Since the former invented three Orders and the latter claimed to have added two more of their own style, why should we not be permitted to follow their example and open up new routes? We certainly have the right to do it and, provided we use it as successfully as the Greeks, we shall deserve to share their glorious fame in this respect. In actual fact, all our efforts have up till now not led to a real invention. One day we shall perhaps see some fortunate man of genius rise and lead us along unknown routes to the discovery of more than one beautiful composition which had escaped the ancients. Let us set our hope on the generosity of nature which probably has not yet shared out all its gifts.

Taking things as they are at present, it seems to me that we have really only three Orders: the Doric, the Ionic and the Corinthian. They alone are distinguished by inventiveness and individual character, whereas the Tuscan and the Composite are nothing more than derivations and differ only incidentally from the other three. The Tuscan is but a cruder version of the Doric and the Composite a rather pleasant blend of the Ionic and the Corinthian. It is therefore true that architecture is only under moderate obligation to the Romans and that it owes everything that is valuable and solid to the Greeks alone. I am not going to speak here about Gothic and Arabesque or Moorish Orders which ruled for too long. They are remarkable only the one for being excessively heavy, the other for being excessively light. Both of them show so little inventiveness, taste and accuracy that they are generally regarded as lasting proof of the barbarism which filled a period of more than ten centuries. Since the rebirth of the fine arts our architects have the noble ambition to immortalize the French name through some new architectural invention. It was Philibert de l'Orme who made the greatest effort to go beyond the bound which, up to his time, had brought architects constantly to a halt. He wanted to give us a new French Order but, although he was otherwise a very able man, more able perhaps than any of the architects who succeeded him, he has shown great lack of imagination in the execution of his project. All it amounts to is a new Composite Order, so misunderstood that it has been given up by everybody. It has been noticed a long time ago that invention is not our strong point. We do better in perfecting and in surpassing the inventions of others.

However that may be, the three Orders alone are our true wealth. The first, the Doric, is the heaviest. Designed for buildings which demand great solidity, its proportions have been regulated in a manner to give it the greatest possible strength without debarring refinement. The last, the Corinthian, is the lightest. Designed for buildings where great elegance is required, its proportions are regulated in a manner to give it the greatest possible refinement without excluding strength. The Ionic keeps to the middle. It is neither as solid as the Doric nor as delicate as the Corinthian; it partakes of one and the other. The three Orders, understood in this way, appear to cover the whole range of art, satisfying all needs and tastes. The Doric and the Corinthian are two extremes beyond which one cannot go without falling into either a clumsy or a fragile style. The Ionic gives us, between these two extremes, the proper and happy medium. There, ingeniously accomplished, is the whole graduation from solid to delicate! It will, therefore, always be extremely difficult to add something new to such a fortunate discovery.

Article I
What All Orders Have in Common

In all Orders the column is composed of three parts: base, shaft, and capital. The pedestals have been proscribed in the last chapter; their fate has been decided once and for all: they will be used for carrying statues, never for carrying columns. It is not the same with the base which must not be left out of any Order because it gives strength to the column from below, increases its solidity and makes the beautiful effect of the diminution and the neck-molding (*congé*) of the column more perceptible. There is no longer any excuse for using a base arbitrarily, once constructional and aesthetic reasons warrant its application. The Doric Order is the only one which originally had columns without base. In the Marcellus Theater, where this Order has been applied, there is no base, and Vitruvius himself does not give a base to the Doric column. These are rather weak authorities to oppose the grounds which make the base a necessary part of all Orders, grounds which are backed by the almost universal practice of ancient and modern architects who adopted the attic base for the Doric Order, just as the other two Orders each have a base of their own.

The entablature is divided in all Orders into architrave, frieze and cornice. Of these three parts only the architrave could and should be used singly whenever there are several stories. The frieze and the cornice can only be used jointly and with the architrave, that is to say that every time a frieze and cornice is applied the whole entablature is needed. Many architects, finding themselves in trouble over the elevation, have taken the liberty to suppress the frieze and to join the cornice to the architrave. This error has been committed unashamedly at the immense building of the Abbey of Prémontré which has to its credit only its vast size, being otherwise a masterpiece of bad taste. This, in my opinion, is a serious fault because without the frieze which has been introduced in a natural way to indicate the space between the components that make up the ceiling and those that form the timberwork, the entablature loses its proportions. Therefore, it is not possible to suppress the frieze without sinning against the rules. This suppression certainly makes a very bad impression and only suggests an architect who has handled dimensions badly. We are faced here with another question which many people do not dare to decide, namely whether the entablature underneath the pediment must be left as a whole. I see that in practice architects follow with indifference one way or the other. According to the true principles, the cornice, which essentially belongs to the roof, must always be eliminated from an entablature which lies under the pediment. Hence the following good effects: (1) The roof will be represented only where the actual roof is; (2) the tympanon of the pediment will no longer be concealed by the great projection of the lower cornice; (3) it will avoid the two cornices meeting in a sharp, acute angle at each end of the pediment, an altogether disagreeable conjunction.

In all Orders, there are two kinds of moldings which are

used for all ornaments, the square and the round. The former are by themselves somewhat harsh and stiff, while the latter are soft and graceful. These moldings, when matched and blended in good taste, give great pleasure. Which then is the right taste for this blending and matching? I venture to make a comparison which is going to clear up this mystery. Round moldings are to architecture what consonances are to musical harmony, whereas square moldings correspond to dissonances. The blending of moldings and of sounds has the same aim and must follow the same rules. The harshness of the dissonances is an artistic device which the judicious composer must use in order to intensify by contrast the charming impression of the consonance. A piece of music would become dull and insipid without the dissonance making itself felt from time to time, though it would grate on the ear if it were too frequent. Hence the rule never to use a dissonance which is not prepared and resolved by a consonance. Let us apply this to architecture where ornaments have a harmony of their own. The round moldings produce softness, the square ones harshness. In order therefore to create perfect harmony, the harshness of the square moldings must from time to time interrupt the softness of the round moldings which could decline into insipid dullness; but it is even more essential that the softness of the latter always corrects the harshness of the former. We should prepare and resolve the dissonance, that is to say every square molding should always be preceded and be followed by a round molding. Then, the work will have nothing of dryness and the whole composition will be an enchanting sight.

In all Orders each single part presents a background on which sculpture can be applied. But here, as anywhere else, confusion and excess must be avoided. Sculpture is to buildings what embroidery is to dresses. When the embroidery is fine and allows enough ground to show through, it adds lustre to the dress and makes it truly stately because it preserves simplicity. When, on the contrary, the embroidery is overloaded and confused, its only merit is richness and labor. Seeing a dress in this way bedecked with embroidery one says: "Here is something which must have cost an immense sum, but is not at all beautiful." Sculpture on buildings demands the same moderation. If care is not taken to distribute it sparingly and in orderly fashion, a great amount will have been spent without achieving anything of value. Architects must therefore beware of covering indiscriminately all parts of an Order with sculpture; restful intervals are needed. If they wish to embellish a work and embellish it judiciously, they should never have two consecutive parts carved; there should always be a plain part to serve as background for a sculptured one. Those who do not keep within these justified bounds will fall into a frivolous, petty style (*colifichet*).

Article II
The Doric Order

The Doric Order will always be favored by architects who love to show their skill venturing upon difficult and thorny paths. It is constrained by limitations not equaled in any other Order and is, therefore, rarely carried out accurately. What makes it so extremely difficult is the succession of triglyphs and metopes which decorate its frieze. Triglyphs must always have the shape of a rectangle, metopes that of a square. This disparity is extremely awkward because it has the result: (1) that Doric columns can never be coupled; to do this it would be necessary for either the bases and even the capitals to penetrate each other or for the metope, which would come between the two coupled columns, to have more width than height, two faults which must never be tolerated;

(2) that one no longer knows how to manage in interior angles where one cannot avoid one of the two drawbacks, namely either to bend a triglyph and thereby mutilate the two adjoining metopes or to join two metopes without any intermediate triglyph. Up till now ignorant people have not been held back by these two difficulties because they were not at all aware of the drawbacks I am talking about. We are not short of buildings using the Doric Order, but there is none where one does not find either folded or half triglyphs or metopes which [are mutilated or][1] are much wider than high. Even the Church of the Novitiate of the Jesuits in the *rue pot-de-fer,* which is rightly counted among our least defective buildings, is a case in point. I do not speak of the much more recent Church of St. Roch where similar errors have been committed with a great deal of license. I shall probably be told that, since these errors are inevitable, one should not make out that those who commit them are criminals. To this I answer that, if occasions exist where these faults are absolutely inevitable, a skillful architect should take scrupulous care to avoid these dangerous occasions. Only at an interior angle can some license be allowed because, after all, it is well-nigh impossible in any building for such an angle not to occur. Therefore, of the two evils the lesser should be chosen, that is the one which is nearer to the natural. In such a case it is, I believe, much better to put up with two square metopes next to each other than to show a folded or half-triglyph.

When it is a question of applying the Doric Order, the architect, fully conscious of the difficulty of the undertaking, should arm himself with perseverance and should make precise studies of this awkward and precarious disparity of triglyphs and metopes. Since the execution cannot be exact without infinite toil, success will be all the more glorious.

The Doric column has the most beautiful and perfect base.

[1]The words in brackets omitted in 2nd ed. (translator's note).

It is the attic or *atticurge* base. The two tori of a different modular size connected by a scotia have a beautiful effect because strength is here joined to grace. This is why architects do not object to borrowing the beautiful base of the Doric and making it the base common to all other Orders. They cannot be blamed for using it in this way; it will always be permissible to take what is excellent in one Order and transfer it to another, provided that one never touches those parts which are the essential characteristics of an Order, since this would merge two Orders into one. This liberty, subject to the limitations I prescribed, in no way contradicts the true spirit of the art; it can even be of great use in making it perfect.

The Doric capital is the plainest and the least elegant of all capitals. A square abacus, an ovolo supported by three annulets, or better still by an astragal and its fillet, followed by a plain member called *gorge* are all its embellishments. Nothing is less ostentatious, nothing in fact more dry and poor! Yet this capital is one of the parts which are the characteristics of the Doric Order and cannot be replaced by another without changing and completely corrupting the character of the Order.

The Doric entablature has its beauty and its faults. The beauty of the entablature consists in the continuous division of the frieze into triglyphs and metopes. It cannot be denied that this arrangement is pleasant and fascinating, especially when the metopes are adorned with reliefs judiciously chosen and carefully designed. The charm of the triglyphs is further enhanced by the mutules which surmount them and which are attached to the soffit. The faults of the entablature are its harshness and its heaviness: its harshness because the square moldings are too often repeated while the round moldings are too few, its heaviness because the fascia of the cornice projects too far. Its wide soffit, weighed down by huge mutules, which have no support at all, seems constantly in danger of tumbling down. The eye is hurt and it wearies the imagination to see these large blocks of stone transported into midair. All these faults, and they are considerable, are ingeniously offset by the remarkable effect produced by the combination of triglyphs and metopes. This effect is so striking that it attracts nearly all attention and one overlooks everything else in favor of such a beautiful invention.

Let us examine this entablature in detail. Its architrave is very plain; only the guttae hanging from below the triglyphs are noteworthy. According to proper practice these guttae should always be in the shape of a square pyramid and it is considered an abuse to make them spherical. Our only guide here is visual judgment and I do not know why guttae in the shape of a square pyramid should be more effective than spherical guttae. The frieze of the entablature is the most beautiful part of the whole Order. There must always be a triglyph in line with the axis of each column because these triglyphs represent the ends of the beams or perhaps rather of the rafters and it is natural that these ends rest on their support. Furthermore, the proper way is to have an uneven number of triglyphs in the intercolumniations. In common practice, architects hardly trouble about this point; this, however, means carelessness and those aspiring to true perfection should not indulge in any carelessness. In the case of a projecting angle it is unavoidable to place a half-metope at the two sides of the corner. Proper practice demands that when the metopes are decorated with reliefs the half-metopes at the projecting angle remain plain so that they do not offer the spectacle of a folded relief. About the cornice I have only one thing to say, namely that the soffit of the fascia, being divided into mutules and lozenges, is subject to the same restrictions as the frieze. The mutules must be decorated with thirty-six round guttae in the shape of small cones. The lozenges can have sculptural decoration. Angles will always be awkward here. There will be no difficulty in recessed angles if one adheres to what I have said before, but at projecting angles the space between the mutules near the corner will have more length than width at both sides. The proper practice therefore demands that on the soffit of the fascia, above the two half-metopes of the projecting angle, there is a rectangle at both sides so that the remaining space at the corner becomes a square and serves as ground for the lozenge.

I shall not go into the details of proportions; they are to be found, stated clearly and accurately, in M. de Cordemoy's *Traite d'architecture* and M. Perrault's *Vitruvius*. For the detailed proportions of each Order I refer to these authors, my aim being no more than to indicate in each Order matter of interest regarding taste.

Many architects have felt the inconvenience of the Doric cornice and some of them have decided to substitute the Ionic cornice for it or to invent a fancy one which is less protruding and less heavy. F. Martel-Ange has given an example of this in his Church of the Novitiate of the Jesuits. I am far from condemning an easing of rules that is so reasonable; but, then, an architectural composition like that is not, strictly speaking, a Doric Order anymore; it becomes a sort of Composite of which I shall speak later on.

Article III
The Ionic Order

The Ionic Order, lighter and more delicate than the preceding one, has the advantage of being almost faultless, although but for this it is without really outstanding qualities. There is no longer the *je ne sais quoi* of the firm and masculine style that distinguishes the Doric and not yet the opulence and magnificence typical of the Corinthian. Its features are those of an average beauty which please because of their regularity, being neither too coarse nor too fine, neither strikingly good nor strikingly bad, but where reign a harmony so perfect and a gentleness so attractive that while unlikely to astonish and enchant they are perhaps more certain to interest and please. The essential merit of the Ionic consists, therefore, in a certain moderate enjoyment, in a charm not spoiled by any appreciable imperfection. Let us go into details.

Vitruvius has given a base to the Ionic Order which, in my opinion and that of many others, is the only thing that could be eliminated. This base is ill-formed and clearly offends against the true principles of nature. The great torus which is supported only by two weak scoties interrupted by two slight astragals, is dreadfully defective. According to good rules, the heaviest part must always be at the bottom, the lightest at the top. This natural order is reversed here and consequently solidity suffers. This base, far from diminishing towards the top, is on the contrary diminished towards the bottom. Narrower near the plinth, it widens out unnaturally where it joins the shaft of the column. These faults, which are real and glaring, have persuaded most ancient and modern architects to proscribe the Ionic base of Vitruvius and substitute for it the beautiful attic base of which we spoke in the preceding article, and in this respect their example cannot be too faithfully imitated.

The Ionic capital is the part of the Order where inventiveness reigns supreme and which marks the character of the Order most vividly. An astragal, an ovolo, an *écorce* which coils into a volute at both ends and is surmounted by an ogee and an abacus are the whole adornment. The great beauty of this capital lies in the two volutes which flank it in an infinitely graceful manner. Formerly the capital had only two of its opposite faces decorated with volutes and the two others with two balusters joined in the center by a pinecone, called *ceinture* or *baudrier*. This diversity causes no inconvenience so long as the face with volutes is to the front, but when, at the first corner, the portico turns at right angles, the capital of the corner column inevitably presents the face with the baluster towards the front. All this necessarily leads to two inconvenient situations: either the capitals of a whole line of columns have to present as frontal view the faces with the baluster, which can only have a very bad effect, or the capitals of the two corner columns present a different face to all other capitals, which was the usual practice though it could not fail to be strangely out of tune. The ancients did not know how to prevent this inconvenience of the Ionic capital. We are indebted to Scamozzi for having made this charming capital more perfect. It was his invention to change it into one with four identical faces, all with volutes. From that time on the capital has lost its awkwardness. The modern have brought Scamozzi's invention to perfection. He retained the square abacus and gave the connecting link between the volutes the same width throughout. The moderns had the idea of making its width in such a manner that the lower side widens out; they also indented and curved the abacus by making it follow the contour of the volutes. The capital, shaped like this, is as graceful as it could possibly be and I do not see how anything more could be added to its perfection.

The Ionic entablature matches the elegance and simplicity of all the rest. Its architrave is divided into three fasciae, each of a different height; it begins with the smallest and finishes with the largest, which is happily crowned by an ogee. The frieze is commonly quite plain, but can also have carved decoration depending whether *bienséance* demands the Order be more or less enriched. The cornice is charming; it has only a moderate projection and this projection is furthermore made unobtrusive by the parts which support the fascia in such a natural way that it does not look perilous or sharp-edged. It is composed of an ogee, a dentil, an astragal, an ovolo, a fascia, an ogee, and a doucine. Among them are few square members and consequently there is nothing that is harsh or dry. Dissonances are rare; they are correctly prepared and resolved, and as a consequence a gentle harmony reigns over the whole.

It should be noted that the cornice has two members which mark the essential character of the Ionic Order. The first is the course of dentils always cut to form a row of small blocks (*taillé en dents*), the second is the fascia with its soffit hollowed out.

The Ionic cornice is without comparison the best composed and the most becoming of all cornices. It has only simple ornaments but is on the other hand of a lightness, ease, and harmony which makes it in many respects preferable to all others. Therefore, good architects hardly ever fail to select it when the disadvantages of other cornices happen to constrain them and when their motives are capable of excusing and even justifying this license.

Article IV
The Corinthian Order

At last we have arrived at the greatest, the most majestic and most sublime architectural creation. The Corinthian Order presents one of those striking sights which, once seen, immediately grips and lifts up the soul into ecstasy. When well carried out, this Order is destined to make a great impression by its noble character and the grand style of its ornaments. The ancients have only known three graces; our three Orders each have their own. Simplicity is the share of the Doric, gentleness distinguishes the Ionic, noble grace belongs to the Corinthian.

Vitruvius gives a base to this Order which is indeed less defective than the Ionic base, but still has great imperfections. It is the Ionic base increased by a great torus immediately above the plinth. The great fault of this base is that it is much too delicate and lacks that look of solidity which is so appropriate and necessary for a base. Its moldings are so fine that at the least stress they must break. Let us therefore come back to our charming attic base which alone is free from all faults and is devised in a highly sensible manner.

The Corinthian capital is a masterpiece and it is mainly by this part that the Corinthian Order stands well above the others. It has perfect grace and great splendor. It consists of a large vase covered by an abacus the four sides of which are curved. The lower part of the vase is covered by two rows of leaves with curved tips that protrude moderately. From the midst of these leaves rise stalks or caulicoles which form small volutes at the corner of the abacus and at the four centers. Everything in this composition is admirable: the vase which serves as ground on which the leaves are artistically arranged; the curvatures and gradually increasing projection of the leaves; the stalks which rise naturally and in their flexibility seem to lend themselves to the workman's aim of bending them into volutes, thus giving to the ledge of the abacus a most elegant support. Over the whole arrangement reigns such a gentleness, harmony, natural ease, variation and grace that in vain would I try to express in words that for which taste alone can give the feeling. M. de Cordemoy rightly condemns the prevailing habit of our architects of using laurel and olive leaves in preference to acanthus leaves and reserving the latter for the Composite capital. I cannot understand what foundation this custom can have except that of a blind caprice. The acanthus leaf has by nature the contour and curves which suit the leaves of the Corinthian capital. This plant grows tender stalks among its leaves which convey quite naturally the caulicoles of the capital and which

these caulicoles with their extension into volutes originally
represented. Everybody knows the story of the sculptor Callimachus. The first idea of the Corinthian capital came to him
by chance when he discovered the vase around which an
acanthus plant had casually grown its foliage and its stalks.
Why do we take pleasure in spoiling the most fortunate idea
that ever was? The small leaves of the laurel or the olive tree,
because of the way they are arranged, can only forcibly be
adapted to the composition of the Corinthian capital. To
substitute them for the large acanthus leaves means abandon-
ing the natural to run after the frivolous, means expressing a
grand thought in a feeble and puerile phrase.

[*Speaking of the Corinthian capital the author of the*
Examen *suggests that we owe its success only to the force of
an old habit and that we would have been deprived of its
elegant decoration if the Greeks had followed a fastidious
feeling* (délicatesse), *seemingly well founded, and had given
in to a too servile adherence to the laws of nature. This
opinion is influenced by the preconceived notion of some
architects who assume that the form of the Corinthian capital
is contrary to solidity. I am far from thinking the same. The
vase which forms the inner core of the capital is a solid body
that has all the necessary strength to carry the abacus and the
architrave. The acanthus leaves and the caulicoles covering
the vase do not completely hide it from view. It shows as
much as is needed to reassure the imagination which would
be startled to see an abacus resting on simple leaves and
stalks. These delicate leaves do not carry anything. The
inventor of this capital has wisely made the curves very
perceptible so that one cannot doubt that they are here as an
ornament only. It is, therefore, quite wrong of the author of
the* Examen *to say: "I know how impossible it would be
today for similar inventions to succeed and I would never
advise any of our artists to risk them unless the* sublime
charm *of the subject throws a veil over the faults and shuts*

the eyes to what is natural to see only what is agreeable." For
my part I fervently wish that we had artists able to produce
inventions which could be on a par with that of the Corin-
thian capital. I dare guarantee them success. As long as they
do not imagine anything more extravagant than this superb
capital they will never transgress the barrier of rules and
nature. Had the author of the Examen *lived at the time of*
Callimachus he would probably have denounced this ingen-
ious innovator as a detestable corruptor of la bonne architecture *and if he had had as much authority as ill humor we*
would have no Corinthian capital. Fortunately, the Greeks
were less exacting; we will be like them every time that artists
can shake off the yoke of dull routine by inventions of such
perfect quality.]

The Corinthian entablature closely resembles the Ionic, but
its ornaments are more diversified and its cornice is not
nearly as perfect. The architrave is divided into three fasciae,
unequal in height as in the Ionic, but each of these fasciae is
adorned by a molding: the first is crowned by an astragal,
the second by an ogee, the third by both these moldings
together. This architrave is the most perfect of all. There is
nothing harsh about it; everything proceeds by graduation.
The frieze can either be quite plain or serve as a ground for a
great piece of sculpture; in this respect it is very much like
that of the Ionic. The cornice is made up by a fascia which
must never be cut *en dents*, an astragal, an echinus or ovolo,
modillions, their upper side crowned by an ogee, a fascia, an
ogee and a doucine. The composition of this cornice is
without harshness, its square moldings are always preceded
and followed by a round molding. The only drawback of this
cornice is its great projection. This soffit of the fascia is
almost as heavy looking as that of the Doric Order. I admit
that it is nicely embellished by the mixture of modillions and
square caissons filled with a sculptured rose or rosette, but,
after all, it is really a *plat-fond* where the modillions, which

support it, conceal a little and yet expose too much the perilous overhang. The doucine surmounting this wide *platfond* increases the projection of the whole cornice even more. Therefore, some architects have decided, when their Corinthian Order is on a great scale, to suppress the doucine. This suppression becomes necessary to avoid the excessive load, but then the cornice thus mutilated does not retain its proportions: terminated by a fascia which is surmounted by a simple ogee it loses a great part of its grace, while its top has become too meager and too flat. I deliberately point out all the disadvantages to be met with when composing architectural Orders, even though the rules are strictly followed, so that architects may become convinced that this beautiful art has not yet reached the perfection of which it is capable and that those among them who are gifted will, on reflection, use their talent to bring about complete perfection. This is an aim which the academies of architecture should keep before them; it would be good if they would offer rewards to those who would devise means by which the faults of which I have spoken will disappear without true beauty being affected. Had they realized there was a service to be given many of our architects would have had enough ingenuity to succeed. Too much have they confined themselves to imitating the ancients instead of bringing to a final conclusion ideas which the ancients through indolence or lack of intelligence have often not investigated sufficiently.

Until my demands on this point be fulfilled, I will observe that the modillions must be so arranged that one of these is always in line with the axis of each column. No dentils are cut out in the Corinthian Order because of the modillions higher up. Everybody knows that the reason for this is derived from the rules of carpentry. In practice most architects break away from this constraint. They probably believe that by multiplying and intermingling all ornaments they make their work more beautiful. Concerning modillions, their peculiar position on the Maison Carrée at Nîmes is well known—they are wrongly placed here. Although this building is one of the most precious remains of good antiquity, one must take great care not to copy this fault which obviously goes against nature. This example proves once more that the ancients were not always and not in everything models to be relied on.

From all I have said it is easy to conclude that each of the three Orders has a character of its own and that although there is a great resemblance between them, they differ from each other in characteristic details. Apart from proportions, with which I do not deal, they each have their own capital and entablature without counting their bases which, strictly speaking, can be different. In practice, an architect must investigate the differences between the Orders very closely so as not to confuse their characteristics; nothing would more expose his ignorance and lack of experience, unless he intended to design a sort of Composite Order of which I shall speak in the following article.

Article V

The Different Kinds of Composites

Architects who lack inventiveness have always been at liberty to make their work more varied through fancy compositions. The three Orders are like a mine from which they can draw to create something valuable embracing a thousand different combinations, products of their taste and talent. The Romans have made use of this liberty, not only for the Composite the proportions and character of which Vitruvius has transmitted to us, but also for many other Composites, traces of which are preserved in ancient monuments. They were not always very fortunate in this kind of arbitrary combinations. I remember having seen fragments of an extremely bizarre cornice among the antiquities discovered a few years ago at the fountain in Nîmes. It may be sufficient for me to say that it shows two distinct fasciae with two rows of dentils and modillions one above the other. This repetition is of bad taste almost without parallel.

Those of our architects who want to design imaginative Composites must take great care to harmonize the parts in such a manner that nothing shocks common sense and that they always follow the usual rules; in this way charm is joined to solidity. For this genre Vitruvius's Composite can serve as model. It shows how one can adapt the essential parts of each Order so as to make an entirely new one which acquires its own character. However, this Composite still has faults which we shall carefully note so that they will be avoided.

The Vitruvian Composite has the same base as the Corinthian but in some parts differs from it distinctly. It consists equally of a vase covered by two rows of acanthus leaves, arranged in the same way as on the Corinthian; but instead of the stems or caulicoles there are fleurons stuck to the vase and twisted towards the center of the capital. The vase is terminated by a fillet, an astragal and an ovolo. From the inside of this vase rise great volutes similar to those of the Ionic Order. These volutes are decorated with a large acanthus leaf which rolls back as if to support the corners of the abacus and from which lower down the fleuron descends along the edges of the volute almost covering it. The abacus is very much like that of the Corinthian capital. The Composite capital has neither the same refinement (*délicatesse*) nor fineness)*légèreté*) as the Corinthian but is even richer and, admittedly, has, as a whole, something grand and pleasing about it. The beauty of this capital has made the Composite extremely famous. There have even been people of little understanding (*peu d'esprit*) who dare to prefer it to the

Corinthian. People of good taste have always taken care to be on their guard against such undiscerning blindness.

The entablature of the Composite does not match the beauty of its capital. The architrave has only two fasciae of unequal height: the first is surmounted by an ogee, the second by an astragal, an ovolo, and a cavetto. For a part as small as the fascia of an architrave there are too many moldings crammed together. Above all, the cavetto does not look well because it makes the crowning of the architrave too delicate and fragile and because its profile is not at all graceful. The frieze is plain or sculptured like the Corinthian. The cornice consists of an astragal, an ogee, a recessed part made up of two fasciae with two rows of modillions attached to it, the first fascia surmounted by an ogee, the second by a fillet and an ovolo; then follows a fascia with the underside hollowed out, an ogee, and a doucine. This cornice is very heavy with the same part too often repeated. The form of the modillions is awkward and weak. The projection of the fascia beyond the modillions is senseless and makes the application of the modillions altogether superfluous. A great deal of rectification is needed, therefore, to make this cornice perfect, or rather a totally different one should be designed.

I am surprised that our architects did not make greater efforts in inventing Composites in the style of the Vitruvian. A few examples still exist to prove that they have the skill or the will to do it. There are Composites which in conception and arrangement are not labored and well within the ordinary, among them some where all that was done was to bring together the major parts of the different Orders, such as an Ionic cornice on a Doric frieze and architrave or a complete entablature of one Order over the columns of a different Order. The most peculiar Composite Order known to me is the one used on the interior porrch of the Church of the Culture St. Catherine. On a Corinthian column and architrave rises a Doric frieze surmounted by an Ionic cornice.

This Composite is very beautiful because it unites the most splendid parts of the three Orders. However, it has one marked fault; the triglyphs are without their guttae hanging over the architrave which reduces their charm a great deal. It would be desirable for our artists to look further ahead and, by combining the parts that are characteristic of all Orders, give us new capitals, new architraves and new cornices; this is a vast field open to ingenuity and competition. It even seems to me that new moldings could be added to the restricted number already in use. But one should remember always to avoid great projections, moldings which are too fine as well as those which are too harsh, and any frills (*hors-d'oeuvres*). Above all, one must study the right proportions; solidity and grace mainly depend on them.

Article VI
How to Enrich the Various Orders

An Order can be enriched in three ways—through rich material, rich work, or both of them together: through rich material when marble, bronze or gold are used, through rich work when the parts are given sculptural decoration, through both together when sculpture of the finest quality is added to marble, bronze or gold.

Rarely can one use marble, bronze and gold; the cost is too high. It is only for royal buildings and our churches that such materials are at hand. In any case, many things have to be observed about the way to use them. Particular attention is needed to match the various colors of marble according to good taste. One must not be tempted by the value attached to some marbles solely because of their rarity, or believe that a building will be beautiful just because it includes marble that came from far away or from an exhausted quarry. Granite and porphyry are a case in point; their colors are not for these reasons made more attractive. The eye does not know whether a thing is rare or unique; these are qualities it does not value at all. It knows very well, however, if a color is beautiful, and what matters here is to satisfy the eye. By this principle one must rank among the beautiful marbles those with vivid colors and with veins which are well marked and well blended or those the design of which is of some bizarre and lively irregularity. Here roughly are the rules to be followed for arranging marbles in their proper way:

1. White marble without veins should be reserved for places where sculpture is going to be used. The veins of marble always ruin what the chisel has touched; they confuse the outline and produce an uneven reflection of light which is unfavorable to the neatness of the work.

2. Veined white marble must be used for all background, while the varied colored marbles must be reserved for columns, friezes and all inlaid panels.

3. The colors of marble must relate as much as possible to the character of the subject. It would be equally as absurd to use marbles in green, red, yellow or any other brilliant color for a mausoleum as it would be to waste black marble on an altar.

4. Bringing together marbles with colors too glaring should be avoided, and even more so those of one and the same color. Brown in too great abundance makes the work look dismal and dull, while soft colors, used predominantly, make it look cold and insipid. It is, therefore, essential to blend one kind with the other and thus bring out the quality of one to that of the other. This makes for a harmony the consonances of which need careful study.

Decoration in marble always needs to be set off for gilding. Bronze gilding is best but is very expensive. For economic reasons gilded wood or lead is often used. Wood takes gilding well, but the humidity of the marble makes it rot. Lead has not this disadvantage, but never takes gilding well. Gilding must never be used lavishly; there should just be enough to brighten up marbles of dull and heavy colors.

The second manner of enriching an Order is to give its parts sculptural decoration. I have already said that to avoid confusion one must never decorate all parts and that it would be best to do it alternately. Concerning this sculpture it only remains for me to note some details on which success depends. The outlines must be well defined and unaffected. When well defined, the work will have been properly made, when unaffected it will have much grace. The design must be natural. Our artists have for some time been leaning towards an extravagance (*bizarrerie*) which has been the great fashion. All the outlines of their ornaments were willfully distorted. At first this eccentricity did not fail to be successful with a nation as fickle and inconsistent as ours. Had this fashion reigned much longer we would have outdone the mad fancies of Gothic (*arabesque*). Luckily one gets over it and this dangerous epidemic is nearing its end. Modeling in the round must be avoided on sculptured decorations because the bulkiness of massive forms always makes architecture look heavy; one must keep to low relief. The decorations of the Chapel of Versailles may serve as model. The whole design is unaffected, properly defined and of a relief of medium depth, all of which makes for great visual satisfaction.

I have nothing to say about the third manner of enriching an Order. The rules which I have given for the two preceding manners should, taken together, be applied to this one.

Article VII

On Buildings without any Orders

The five Orders are not suitable for every kind of building because they involve expense which not everybody is able to afford and require a facade of a scale feasible for few buildings. The five Orders really only belong to great churches, royal palaces, and public buildings; for all other buildings one must necessarily fall back on much simpler and less costly decoration. Attractive and even beautiful buildings can be built without the help of entablatures and columns. Our architects know that very well and I daresay that it is in this sort of building they ordinarily succeed best. The composition, being much freer and less dogmatic, is equally within reach of a genius and of an architect of average ability. A great architect should not regard this work as beneath him; the freer the composition the easier it is to bring in something that is novel and ingenious, to make it as graceful as one pleases, to embody in the composition all kinds of elegant, noble and sublime thoughts and, what is even more valuable, to vary the design ad infinitum. Thus, a skillful person, applying himself to this task, will always achieve something to be proud of.

The beauty of the buildings I am talking about depends mainly on three things: accuracy of proportions, elegance of forms, and choice and distribution of ornaments.

However free the composition of a facade may be, its proportions are never arbitrary. Of all variations possible for an elevation there is only one which is right for a given length. The spectator, looking at an elevation, will always find it too high or too low until he encounters the one and only ratio which he unconsciously looks for. The artist's skill consists in studying this ratio and grasping it accurately.

[*Incidentally, when I say that of all possible elevations there exists only one good one, I do not maintain that all buildings which have the same length must have the same height, but that all buildings of the same character must have the same height for a given length. What makes up the character of a building is the style* (genre) *chosen and the destination* (destination) *it is intended for. Churches, palaces,*

private houses, corps-de-logis, *pavilions, domes, towers—
there are the various and main styles. Different destinations
give rise to more or less lofty ideas and call for a simple,
elegant, noble, august, majestic, extraordinary or prodigious
manner. When the architect has fully grasped the essence of
the destination by the feeling which arises in his soul, he must
choose the style. This preliminary step demands from him a
lively talent, decisive taste and wise and well-reasoned consideration. Once the destination is known and the style* (goût)
*chosen, the character of the building is fixed. Then I main-
tain that the proportions are not arbitrary anymore and that
necessarily there is only one that is legitimate. My reasoning
is that nature has not two different ways of bringing about an
effect. The effect is more or less satisfying according to how
strictly one adheres to the unique way that leads to it. Thus,
the ratios between height and length of facades are necessarily unchangeable. I say the same of the ratios between
width, height and length in the interior of buildings. The
precise ratio is unfortunately unknown; there has not been
sufficient research to that end. One should start by establish-
ing the greatest and smallest height possible for the proportions of the exterior. These two terms would be the extremes
of a scale the intermediate steps of which would supply all
the middle terms relating to the different characters of buildings. The same procedure should be used for the lengths and
heights of the interior, that is to fix first the smallest and the
greatest terms and then to divide the scale in proportionate
intervals. This research is of the greatest importance; it is
surprising that one pays so little attention to this matter. M.
Briseux has just printed a work in a magnificent way in
which he wastes much time to prove the need for proportions, a need that can only be called into question by those to
whom the first notions of architecture are unknown, a need
that* M. Perraud *(sic) only opposed through a spirit of contra-
diction. He felt the whole absurdity of his paradox which he*

upheld only out of sheet obstinacy. It would have been of greater value if M. Briseux had applied himself to giving us rules which are capable of satisfying enlightened reason and of leading us with certainty to true proportions. What he says about it is founded only on a practice for which he gives but false reasons.

The proportions of each part must correspond to the whole with the same precision. The dimensions of the stories, doors, windows, and of all attending ornaments are to be regulated by the length and height of the whole building and must be so well balanced that the resulting whole pleases. About all this we really have no rule which is well established. The single point which one must attain and beyond which one should not go is not sufficiently known to us. Only natural taste together with great experience can safely guide architects on this obscure path. They come more or less close to this limit according to how subtle their sensibility is or to what extent long practice has made their visual judgment infallible. It would be desirable if critical research were undertaken in this field which in time could arrest uncertainty and determine for every kind of building the precise limit and the exact point of the dividing line between the too high and the too low, between the too great and the too small. This side of the art has been too much neglected. How many buildings are either too thin or too squat, how many elevations of stories, doors, windows, plinths, or cornices on the same building err by either too much or too little! This is one of the most essential parts of art. Any building which has accurate proportions, though it has only this quality and is otherwise of the greatest simplicity, will always be satisfying in its effect. If, on the other hand, proportions are wanting, that is a fault which rich ornaments will never correct, and one will be grieved to hear it said by anybody: "This is too high" or "that is too low."

I mentioned in the second place elegance of forms, This

subject is not to be neglected if one wants to make buildings that please. Forms are determined by plans. The only way to make forms look pleasing is to avoid ordinary and hackneyed plans seeing to it that they always contain something new, ornamental (*historié*) and even uncommon. It will be of help here to take advantage of regular geometrical figures, from the circle to the most elongated ellipse, from the triangle to the many-sided polygon. Shapes can be made up from straight and curved lines; this device makes it easy to vary the plans almost ad infinitum and give each plan a form which is in no way ordinary and yet is always regular. The rectangle is the most common form of our buildings. However, this far too universal form has become hackneyed and is not interest-ting anymore. It is our nature to love novelty and variety; the fine arts must all be adapted to this inborn taste. We value their excellence only in as much as we find in them something that stimulates and satisfies taste. If the examination of most of our buildings makes so slight an impression on us, it can be attributed to the extreme monotony of their plans. He who has seen one has almost seen them all: always a rectangle varying only in size. The Collège des Quatre Nations is virtually the only one of our buildings which is new and uncommon in its shape and, therefore, never fails to attract special attention. On close inspection one will realize that the best quality of this charming building comes from the elegant form and the graceful blending of curved and straight lines in its plan. [*As long as, in order to vary forms, one does not stray from regular geometrical figures, there is never any need to fear falling into extreme extravagance* (bizarrerie). *Things will be made diverse without making them confused.*]

The form of a building can derive elegance of another kind from the different heights given to its various parts and from the manner by which the sculptural decor (*amortissements*) is varied. The Palais de Luxembourg and the Tuileries have this latter kind of elegance through their form and not at all the

65

former one. The great garden facade of the Château de Versailles has neither one nor the other. Towards the court-yards the plan of the Château is slightly more ornamental but is without taste and without elegance. There is a succession of rectangular courts getting narrower from one to the next until the last is so narrow that it is quite shocking. The plan of the stables is really elegant since it has the right mixture of straight and curved lines. If these two stables were joined to the first court by two porticoes in the form of a longitudinal section of an ellipse this part would outshine everything else.

I last mentioned choice and distribution of ornaments. For a simple decoration it is sufficient to mark the corners of a building from top to bottom by quoins and the stories by a plain band projecting slightly, to give doors and windows plain casings, and to have the whole building crowned by an uncomplicated and gracefully designed cornice. Since in decorations of this kind the plain wall must necessarily appear, there are no great objections to making the heads of doors and windows in the shape of a segmental or even semicircular arch. Should richer decorations be wanted, one can mark all the all spaces between the windows (*trumeaux*) with panels of various shapes filled in with decorative bas-reliefs. Carved fleurons can be placed over doors and windows; this is better than marking the keystone with animal masks, consoles or, what is even worse, with cartouches, a type of ornament that can only be in bad taste because there is nothing like it in nature; it would be best never to use it.

All I do here is to offer my views to the architects. It is up to them to follow up, extend and improve what I have indicated. They know now that one can design all kinds of buildings in varying degrees of beauty without employing any of the five Orders. From that they should conclude that even on grand buildings a good way to vary the impression of magnificence is to join to the splendor of the Orders the elegance of buildings without Orders. These then are many resources which I place in their hands. If they understand how to profit hereby, it will be easy for them to embellish and vary everything.

Chapter III
Observations on the Art of Buildings

One must build with solidity, for convenience and according to *bienséance*. This will be the subject of three separate articles.

Article I
On the Solidity of Buildings

Solidity is the first quality a building must have. Frequent reconstruction of a building is too expensive and too disturbing to allow neglect of any precaution capable of assuring the longest possible life. The ancients, anxious to leave traces of their skill to the most distant posterity, spared nothing to give their buildings that strength which triumphs over ordinary accidents. There are now buildings, six or seven hundred years old, that show no sign of decay beyond their brown and blackened color. It is the same with other buildings going back to a time before the establishment of our monarchy with nobody ever attending to their upkeep and repair. Although more than once their destruction and demolition has been attempted, they still exist to our great astonishment and are ready to be admired by those born many centuries after us. Our artists today do not have this great concern for solidity. It is doubtful whether their buildings could withstand the onslaught of three centuries. They are even accused of deliberately avoiding making them last because, it is alleged, they are interested in renovating the work. We certainly come quite frequently across new buildings which threaten to collapse. Is this due to the architect's lack of intelligence or to his sharp practice? It must be one or the other and at times both of them. It would be essential to have regulations in this field so as to prevent, if possible, the public's constantly becoming the dupe of incompetent and dishonest workmen.

The solidity of a building depends on two things: choice of material and its efficient use.

Stone, lime, sand, wood, iron, plaster, brick, tile, and slate are materials necessary for the construction of a building. Nothing is irrelevant to the choice of these materials. It is the architect's duty to know the bad, medium, good, and excellent quality of each kind. Normally, this study is not very difficult. In each country it is more or less known from where the best stone, the best wood, the best iron, etc., come. The integrity of a contractor should be such as not to abuse the good faith of his employers and pass for good what is bad and for excellent what is only mediocre. It is no good to say as an excuse for such a fraud that clients are not willing to agree to the proper price. I could cite many examples where people did agree to the price and even went above it and yet were cheated more than others. Besides, only a mercenary workman for whom profit comes before honor would make this a convenient excuse. From an architect I expect nobler sentiments. I expect him to be a man filled with true love for his art who prefers the glory of having distinguished himself and the happiness of having succeeded to any other reward. A

69

man possessing this laudable ambition will be free of trickery and falsehood. Not wishing to do things by halves he will accurately inform his employers what is best and what is less good, what is indispensable and what is adequate, be it quantity or quality. He will be firmly opposed to senseless economies which, to avoid an immediate slight increase of expense, will in the end only give rise to more cost. He will not take charge of a building unless he is free to use materials for it suitable in quality and quantity. Should he have to reduce the number of his contracts, he will prefer to do less but do it well. As soon as his desire to enrich himself dominates, his sense of honor is corrupted. The arts suffer from this baseness almost as much as morals do. Everything turns on getting hold of money and on deceiving people. During the construction of buildings a mass of detail can become the opportunity for many a theft. Fictitious supplies, bills made out at the highest price for bad materials deliberately chosen, all these are openly charged to the account, a hundred times worse than a pharmacist's bill. There are sensible people who maintain that the fine arts are the ruin of a state. This reproach applies only to greedy artists who deal in the deception of mankind. The desire for gain makes them invent all sorts of false projects; they find fools who accept them and if the client gives in even only a little to their greed, they are capable of draining a kingdom to exhaustion. I think I will be forgiven this digression; it contains blame which artists will find bitter. I have made it without acrimony and solely because of my eager interest. Besides, this criticism falls only on persons who, far from being masters of the art, are just mercenary artisans whom I would never for a moment confound with our true architects.

Materials are not all of the same quality. The aim of an architect's studies must be to get to know their properties and the differences between them and to get so much practice that by only a touch and a brief glance he arrives at a sure judgment and is safe from any fraud by traders. Materials of the same quality are not equally good for every type of work. This too is a matter for discrimination with which the architect must be familiar. He will thus avoid not only grave blunders, since he can ascribe to everything its proper function, but also useless expense since he possesses the secret of turning everything to account. There are parts of a building which must be of good quality, others where a medium one is sufficient and finally others which must be of the very best. Only bad quality must always be rejected. When an architect takes the risk of using it, he soon realizes his error and reproaches himself, but always too late.

Apart from the choice of materials, the way in which they are used also contributes considerably to the solidity of the work. In all buildings distinction must be made between the parts that weigh down and those that give support. A building will have all the solidity needed if the force of load nowhere exceeds the force of support, when the balance between the two is right. Let us consider a detached wall. It is at the same time its own load and support because the upper parts weigh on the lower and the lower parts carry the upper. Now let us examine an entire building. It consists of several walls which carry vaults, ceilings, and a roof. The vaults, the ceilings, and the roof are the load of a building and the walls are their support. The planning architect should correctly estimate the force of loads so as to regulate with certainty the force of supports.

Some loads such as the weight of massive walls which rest directly on their foundations act in a perpendicular direction, that is pressing from the top down; to estimate their load it is enough to measure height and width of the wall. Other loads such as the weight of vaults act in an oblique direction, that is pressing to the right and left; to estimate their load, the convexity of the vault must be measured; the more flattened this is, the stronger is the thrust. Finally, there are the ceilings and the roof which exercise much weight in a perpendicular direction and little thrust in an oblique direction. All this must be very carefully estimated.

The solidity of the building depends, therefore, mainly on the strength of its support. He who knows how to give a simple wall all the necessary strength so that it never gives way is in a position to provide supports that are sufficient for the heaviest loads.

Three things make a wall strong and firm: the foundation on which it rests, its thickness, and the bonding and verticality of all its parts. The best foundation of all is the rock or living stone. However, this can be deceiving. It sometimes happens when digging into the soil that one comes upon surfaces of rock of insufficient thickness. These are natural vaults which are bound to be crushed by the weight of a great wall. When, therefore, the building in question is of considerable size, it is of the utmost importance to probe the thickness of the exposed rock to make sure that it is not hollow or, if there is a cavity, that the vault-like layer (*calotte*) is strong enough to carry extremely heavy loads. In the absence of rock one has to dig down to firm soil or to the undisturbed ground. If water or sand in depth are encounttered, piles must be used, the sort of foundation which is probably the best and the most stable if well done.

It is essential to build on sound foundations, a principle so obvious that it would seem needless to mention it. Nevertheless, grave mistakes, committed in this respect, show how necessary it is to stress this principle repeatedly. Could it be believed that at a building such as St. Peter's in Rome it had been overlooked to make sure of the foundation? A considerable part of this great basilica rests on the ruins of the ancient circus of Nero, and no one took the trouble to dig down to solid ground. Here then is a building which should have been built for eternity exposed to inevitable decay! This was proved when the Cavaliere Bernini planned to erect two bell towers at the two corners of the facade of this church. He erected one of them; the work was not yet far advanced when he noticed dangerous subsidence which the additional weight had brought about at the lower walls. The strength of these walls seemed to be foolproof; it was, therefore, rightly concluded that the fault was caused by the foundation. In order to be sure about it excavations were undertaken which disclosed the defect I am talking about. An attempt was made to rectify it by subterranean supporting walls. This remedy arrested the progress of the evil without striking at its root. Let this example cause our architects to be circumspect and exacting about the quality of the soil they use as foundation. In this connection safety measures cannot be overdone. [*Every day faults of this kind are still committed which are as gross as they are irreparable. Have we not seen the Church of St. Sulpice suffer accidents and fractures in spite of the massive structures that have been used to strengthen this building? It is said that this is not the architect's fault, that since the ground is not equally solid throughout some parts of the building are bound to subside. But why were all the necessary precautions not taken to make sure of the condition of the ground and provide solidity in places where it is lacking? Why is it that ancient buildings are found to be more secure from these unfortunate subsidences than our modern buildings? Should we have come across obstacles which were formerly unknown? Or is it not that the ancients had in this matter greater knowledge and a more correct and truer way of construction than we have?*]

Once the foundation has been well chosen and prepared, the material should be placed in such a way that (1) the level of the courses is accurate and the plumb line perfect; (2) the stones, headers as well as stretchers, keep the same position they had in the quarry; (3) the joints of the lower course are always overlapped by the facing of the upper course; (4) there is no void inside the wall.

The laziness of workmen has introduced in some districts a strange way of building all that part which is underground. Having dug trenches of the required length and breadth they fill these trenches with large stones thrown in any way together with a lot of mortar. This is the worst possible practice. Apart from its being unavoidable that great gaps remain inside a filling done so haphazardly, the stones thrown in carelessly will land in all sorts of wrong positions, some lying on their narrow, others on their long edge; they will inevitably be crushed by the heavy mass put on top. Subsidence and cracks will be the result. It is not true that masonry which is going to remain underground does not require the same accurate workmanship as that which is going to be exposed to the eye. To make a good foundation one must make use of ashlar or at least of large stones of regular size. All must be done with the help of level, measuring rod, and plumb line. Too much mortar must be avoided. As soon as mortar is used for any other purpose than that of binding the stones and filling in the very small spaces which remain between them, mortar is bound to look unsightly. To be good a wall must be evenly strong throughout. This is not so when there are wide stretches of mortar between the stones. Rules for the best manner of building will be found in M. Perrault's *Vitruvius.* If models are needed the Observatoire and the new buildings of the Louvre provide excellent ones.

For a building to be solid the walls must be of reasonable thickness. This thickness is subject to rules which are generally found in architectural treatises; for that reason there is no need for me to talk about it. I shall only examine whether, with very high walls, it is necessary or immaterial to have every story recessed. These recesses are very common although it seems to me that there is no need for them. If the wall is built according to rules and is perfectly perpendicular, it will be all the more solid even when its thickness is the same from top to bottom. I admit that it is extremely difficult to keep to this precision of verticality throughout all parts of a big wall. There are, it is true, some very encouraging examples among ancient buildings of exorbitant heights. But our workmen can only look at them in wonder and since they lack the grand ambition of imitating what they admire and of being equal to their predecessors of old, they will probably hold on to their imperfect routines forever. As things are, it is therefore safer to build with recesses, taking care always to make them the same on each side of the wall so that the weight rests precisely in the center.

The thickness of the walls must be limited. It is important not to attach anything superfluous, for one thing in order to avoid too heavy an expense but, mainly, in order not to fall into a heavy and massive style. The two extremes are equally faulty. However, if one has to choose, excessive lightness would be preferable to the huge masses too often, and certainly quite unnecessarily, to be met with in modern architecture. The great secret of true perfection of the art consists in joining solidity to *délicatesse*. Whatever our artists say, these two qualities are not at all incompatible. In buildings of the Gothic style *délicatesse* has sometimes been taken as far as it can go, even beyond the generally accepted limits. These buildings have not had less solidity than ours; the fact that they have lasted so long vouches for it. I wish that at least in this respect architects would adopt the spirit of this ridiculous style and study the astonishing workmanship of this way of building where nothing gives way although everything is extremely fine. The old buildings of the Abbey of St. Denis were in this respect far superior to the new ones. Even lesser connoisseurs regret that so much money has been spent to replace a work which was *délicatesse* itself with heavy walls like those of a fortress. The contrast of a new building next to the old church will prove for a long time that the workmen of the eighteenth century came nowhere near the skill of those of the eleventh and twelfth centuries. The Church of St. Sulpice is another monument where the coarseness of our work has, unfortunately, been sanctioned. Did it need such heavy masses to give solidity to this building? Our architects will assert this, the public will be against them and I would only have to take them to Sainte Chapelle to confound them. The ancients were sparing with the use of stone and lavish with that of iron; in this way and with the help of level and plumb line they succeeded in joining the solid to the delicate. What would be the disadvantage of doing as they did? We understand decoration infinitely better than they did, but they were more skilled in construction than we are. If we want to improve, do not let us consult them in matters of decoration but let us never stop consulting them in those of construction.

[*Shall we never see an architect brave enough to rise above the false prejudices learned in the schools of architecture? The timid attitude of the teachers instills into their pupils nothing with greater care than the necessity of increasing the mass to make the buildings solid. This submissive fear, caused primarily only by lack of practice and knowledge, is traditionally transmitted from one set of pupils to the next. The public may well groan at the useless waste of stones which hurts their eyes and empties their purse; they may well appeal to the example of the Gothic buildings: they are told that they are ignoramuses and that no way exists of improving matters. May at last a bold and fearless genius arise who will free our buildings of all the superfluous masses and teach the workmen, superstitious slaves of a bad practice, that nothing was done in the past that could not be done again.*]

Vaults exert thrust to the right and left and thus call for an additional force in the supporting walls. Until now, nothing better has been devised to prop them up than buttresses or flying buttresses; they prevent the walls from moving aside. To that purpose they are used on churches which are really the only buildings with great vaults liable to exert a heavy thrust by their weight as well as by their height. These buttresses, which unfortunately are unavoidable, make the outside of our churches unsightly. I shall explain later on my idea about the course that could be taken to hide them from view. What I have to point out now regarding the great vaults is that one must try to diminish their weight as much as possible. There are two useful means of achieving this. The first is to trace accurately the curve of the vault, the second to give it moderate thickness. Accurate tracing contributes greatly to the solidity of vaults and helps to ease the support. Those who know the science of stonecutting do wonders at small cost. Not only is it easy for them to execute vaults which are so flattened that they resemble proper ceilings, but also they discover the secret of holding up great masses of stone in the air without the appearance of any vault. There are structures, like the staircase of Prémontré, the boldness of which has something frightening about it and is made possible only through the knowledge of stonecutting. Therefore, an architect cannot work too hard to gain so precious a knowledge, the most mysterious part of architecture. For its perfect understanding the work of P. Derrand, S.J., will be of great help. [*It is to be hoped that his* Traite de la coupe des pierres *will be given a better form. Apart from the fact that the language is a little out of date, the subject matter has not been treated with sufficient precision and lucidity and not at all exhaustively. M. de la Rue has worked on the same subject but while he has corrected some inaccuracies of P. Derrand he has added very little to his discoveries. On this subject many points remain to be discussed and many difficulties to be removed.*]

The second way of building light vaults is to reduce their thickness. Examining the vaults of Gothic buildings one will find that most of them are hardly six inches thick. Is it necessary to make them thicker? On the contrary, it seems to me they could be made even less thick. We have recently learned of excellent vaults having the thickness of a single brick. This invention, old in some countries and new for us, shows that a vault does not need to be thick in order to be solid. Let us benefit from this discovery and there will always be so much the less to carry.

[*M. le Comte d'Espie has just published a very instructive little book on how to construct the vaults I am talking about. He cites various experiments carried out to establish the solidity of these vaults which can be given any desired form but which usually are constructed in the shape of a very shallow curve imitating a ceiling* en impériale. *The experiments dealt with in the book I quoted prove clearly that these vaults have no thrust whatsoever. This advantage, once established, would alone be enough to prefer them to any other kind of vault. The other advantages are unquestionable: lightness, saving of wood, and safety from all accidents by fire. It is essential that the public takes note of the value of this new method. It will cost little to make sure by repeated tests whether the facts put forward are true. It is in their favor that they have been in use in the Roussillon for a very long time and that recently similar vaults were successful both in the Languedoc, where they are at present quite common, and at Bisi where the Maréchal de Belle-isle had them constructed.*

All consists in having good bricks and good mortar. These two materials joined together make such a strong bond that they cannot be parted anymore except by breaking them up. The device of these vaults is very simple: no more curve is needed than is necessary to outline the shape of the vault. The workman makes a groove in the walls at the level from which the vault is to rise. Into this groove he places a first row of bricks as stretchers all the way round; he binds them together with mortar which, having set almost immediately, holds the bricks up without any other support and forms one

78

body with them. From this first course the workman carries on with the second course along the outline of the curve making sure that the joints do not meet, and continues in this way up to the keystone. Gradually the vault is formed, held up by bonding alone. It has the thickness of only one ordinary brick, yet is so solid that, unless it is broken up with a hammer, the vault will not give way under the heaviest load. However, for greater safety one doubles it by placing a second layer of bricks as a cover over the first. The haunches of the vault are strengthened on their outside curve by an abutment of bricks that rises from the wall and rests against the vault itself.

A vault thus stiffened is of foolproof strength and if it is true that it has no thrust at all is of invaluable usefulness. The proof of its not having any thrust is the fact that it does not require thick supporting walls. These vaults hve been constructed on simple partition walls only four inches thick. What an advantage, above all in our churches, if with such vaults which admit all kinds of ornaments we save the ordinary cost of thick walls and free ourselves from the annoying servitude to buttresses.

The same author who informs us of all these interesting details has invented the construction of roofs with simple bricks without putting in a single piece of timber. This invention which he has executed at his own house in Toulouse very much deserves to be studied thoroughly. The same principle of construction as that of the vaults gave him the idea of these roofs where bricks bound with mortar make one body and form the pitch of the roof on which it is then easy to lay tiles or slates. It is not difficult to see how much roofs like that would reduce costs, increase the solidity of roofing, and protect it from all accidents by fire.

This method that would exclude from buildings all timber which up to now had been considered necessary can be appreciated only by those who know the price of timber in

France and the various dangers which are unavoidable with its use in buildings. It is, therefore, very desirable that an unbiased examination of the possibility of this new method is undertaken. Once the public has spoken in its favor, the workmen will soon get used to it.]

It is also right to point out that in whatever way a building has been constructed, if it is intended to last, good care must be taken never to weaken the support. Massive bulk is sometimes deceptive. One assumes that it contains something excessive and superfluous, concludes that by taking away a little no harm will be done and will soon regret seeing the whole building crumble. These faults are usually committed when planning to disengage or decorate a building. The Cavaliere Bernini was certainly a great man but he committed this fault in a most fateful manner. A foolhardy desire to decorate made him confident enough to hollow out the four huge pillars which carry the dome of St. Peter's in Rome. These masses seemed to lend themselves to some reduction, but the experiment showed that there was nothing in excess. Since they have been weakened, the vault of the dome has cracked in several places; one will have all the trouble in the world to prevent its ruin. [*I know that the followers of Bernini left nothing undone to acquit him of such a grave accusation. But whatever they may say the cracks in the dome which were not noticed until work was done at the massive pillars and which have continuously grown wider leave him under strong suspicion.*]

Once a building is finished it is always dangerous to interfere with it. It should be assumed that its architect knew his metier, put into the building only what was absolutely necessary, and made each thickness commensurate to the quantity and quality of the loads. It is much better to be wrong in this assumption than to risk destroying the whole. Reports by experts should not be trusted too much; several know little about it and some are so dishonest as to give false

assurances about the dangers they pretend to disgard because, far from suffering loss, they will definitely profit by
them.

To prevent all the rogueries, so familiar to contractors,
these people must know, once and for all, that they can hope
for no immunity. A law which would force them to repair at
their own expense all damage suffered by the building, except
that by accident extraneous to their metier, and which would
constrain them through arrest and confiscation of their prop-
erty, would be the most necessary and wisest of all laws.

Article II

On Convenience

Buildings are made to be lived in and only inasmuch as they
are convenient can they be habitable. Three things contribute
to the convenience of a dwelling: the situation, the planning,
and the internal communications (*dégagements*).

The situation is either open or enclosed. If it is open, a
place must be chosen having good air and a fine view. Health
is always affected by bad air; a dull view deepens or causes
melancholy. It is therefore of great consequence to decide on
a situation—provided one is free to choose—which combines
healthy air with a pleasant view. Air is really only healthy
when it is neither too dry nor too humid. Too much dryness
is bad for the chest, too much humidity is the cause of a
thousand misfortunes. In mountainous places there is no need
to be afraid of humid air; there, however, the air is too sharp
and too rough, one is battered by the wind, usually lacks
water and has constantly to climb up and down. Situations
like this have obviously many inconveniences. Down in valleys
or plains one breathes soft air, but it is humid and marshy; in
winter there is constant fog, while in summer the place is

polluted by foul smells and beset by insects. Situations like this are again very inconvenient. A place sufficiently high to dominate the plain with no marshes or brackish waters near it, sheltered from strong winds by some nearby forest or mountain and near to a pretty stream without fear of flooding—such a place would be very healthy for a dwelling. If, moreover, it had a view over a fertile plain, full of a variety of objects, which does not stretch too far but was pleasantly bound by hills of moderate elevation, one would enjoy the advantages of a view well suited to stimulate the imagination. It is astonishing that our kings to whom nothing is impossible have chosen one of the dullest places of nature for their regular residence. Versailles has cost immense sums of money, but because of its situation and in spite of all artistic efforts at embellishment it casts gloom over all who live there. I do not even know if the air is healthy there in view of the water around it. Astonishment grows when one sees St. Germain to which nature has refused nothing; with much less cost it would have been easy to create an enchanting residence there.

[*As far as the situation is concerned the Château de Belle-vue has all the advantages to be desired. Here all the charm and the magnificence befitting a royal house could easily be brought together. All it needs is to enlarge the plateau and to extend it as a terrace to Meudon on one side and to St. Cloud on the other. This would make it possible to add to the building all necessary extensions. On this long terrace given the shape of a* fer-à-cheval *one could arrange the gardens and bosquets in a delightful manner. Down to the lower terrace sloping gardens could be laid out, with pools* (nappes d'eau) *and cascades here and there; the uneven ground would give rise to the most attractive diversity. High up behind the Château one could plant trees which in this position and through their green foliage would increase the charm of such a beautiful place. One could bring the waters of the Seine in a canal direct from Paris to a point below Bellevue. This canal could be lined on both banks with an avenue of four rows of trees and would offer as vista the Dome des Invalides. To get from the bottom of the hill to the plateau there could be on both sides of the canal a road which, rising gently, would make carriage access easy. A royal house, arranged in this way and presenting itself, as it were, like a fan* (en éventail), *would give Paris a superb viewpoint and Paris would do the same for Bellevue. Paris and the Court, being in close proximity and always in view of each other, would enjoy their mutual fêtes without having to change places; their relations, so necessary in every respect, would be that much easier.*]

In towns it is not always possible to choose a situation which has the advantages I have just mentioned. The site causes difficulty; it can never be large in size nor of a perfectly regular shape. Only the quarter and the street can be freely chosen. In view of this restraint one must at least decide on the best aired and cleanest quarter and the widest and best aligned street because access is easier and the air more readily renewed. In short, the convenience of the locality depends on the great number of circumstances to which particular attention should be given. It must have water, must be within reach of places where the necessities of life can be had, and must be away from noise. Entrance and exit must be easy. Windows must be effective and they cannot be so if there is not an open space in front. I recall all these things only in order to instruct those who have the means to realize them which is not the case with the mass of the people.

Once the site has been chosen, the position of the building remains to be decided and this means finding the best protection against too much cold and too much heat. Generally speaking, east and west are two uncomfortable positions; in summer people are scorched by the sun which shines almost half the day. North is too cold and always a little humid. South seems to be the best position. In winter the sun shines and reduces the cold, in summer it skims the walls and does not give too much heat. However, in every country there is usually one part of the horizon from which strong winds and constant rains come; if one wants to be comfortably housed, good care must be taken not to turn the house towards such a troublesome part of the sky; it must face the opposite direction. The convenience of the position depends on many other circumstances relating to the climate, none of which an architect ought to ignore.

Next to a favorable situation it is exterior and interior planning that contributes most to the convenience of a building. Exterior planning has as its object the arrangement of entrances, courtyards, and gardens. A building is always inconvenient if there is not at least one courtyard which the coaches can enter and where they can turn round with ease. It is deprived of a great convenience when it has no garden. A garden in town is a great amenity, if only to have fresh air and some greenery; what is even more pleasing is to be able to stroll in one's own ground not having to go elsewhere, where one can be at any time *en déshabille*, avoid unwelcome encounters, and see only those one wants to see. If the site is large enough to provide for a courtyard and a garden, one should get both, taking all possible care to turn the garden towards the side where neighbors cannot overlook it. To achieve convenience by exterior planning it is necessary to observe the following: (1) The main *corps de logis* should be placed at the far end of the courtyard and face the garden; in this way one will be safe from noise and have plenty of air and light. (2) The main entrance to the street should be in the center of the courtyard and those to the *corps de logis* and the garden should be in exactly corresponding positions; on this depends the ease of entering and leaving. (3) Next to the main courtyard at least one other courtyard should be provided where the garbage of the stables, the kitchen and the whole house may be collected; this stableyard must have its own exit to the outside on which depends the cleanliness which greatly affects the purity of the air. (4) The ground floor of the main *corps de logis* should be raised by some steps above the pavement of the courtyard and the garden; this rise is necessary to give protection from damp.

A practice has been introduced contrary to what I have just said about the entrance to the *corps de logis*. Many people no longer want it anymore to be in the center because they say it means giving up the best room in the house in order to turn it into a vestibule which is after all only a place to pass through. Therefore, they decide to move the entrance into one of the corners or to one of the wings. This idea has always shocked me. It results in a great inconvenience; a stranger, entering the courtyard, is obliged to ask for the entrance to the house. Once the doorway has been placed in a corner it becomes necessary for the sake of symmetry to simulate an identical one at the opposite corner. Consequently, someone who does not know about it must feel uncertain, not knowing where the real and where the blind entrance is. No doubt, it will be said that this is a slight inconvenience compared to the advantage of having an apartment that occupies the whole width of the *corps de logis* and is no longer interrupted by a vestibule. I admit that this advantage is quite attractive. But, as a consequence, the place for the entrance to the garden can then only be arranged in a way which is awkward or annoying. One will have to do one of two things: either one has to pass through the apartment in order to enter the garden from the center or enter it directly but only from the corner. I go further and say that entrances in the corner of the courtyard look mean and unpleasant. They imply that one is cramped for space and forced to make use of the room which should have been the vestibule in order to enlarge the apartment. Besides, since the natural function of a doorway is to be the common outlet of the whole *corps de logis*, its normal location is the center from which it communicates equally with all outlying parts.

The entrance to the Château de Versailles is placed with little care. The visitor, standing in the courtyard, notices at its end a very small *corps de logis* with three large openings. He advances confidently believing that this is the entrance to the Château. On arriving there, he finds a vestibule into which he has to descend and which moreover connects with nothing. Seeing the garden in front of him, he looks around for a door and, wishing to go up to the *appartements*, for a staircase; but there is nothing there, so that, if he does not make sure of a guide, he will be a long time guessing where the entrance is.

Interior planning affects the comfort of the accommodation even more than exterior planning and demands attention down to the smallest detail. Supposing the entrance door to be in the center and the *corps de logis* to have a floor above the ground floor; then the staircase must be seen clearly from the entrance and must be so placed that nothing obscures it and the staircase does not itself obscure anything. The proper way to place it is at the side of the vestibule and whenever possible on the left side because it is natural to mount with the left foot first. A staircase placed directly in the center and in line with the entrance door is bound to lead to a great deal of inconvenience, as is proved by the staircase of the Luxembourg which is arranged in this way. Apart from other defects, such as its clumsiness and lack of light, it fills up the place of the vestibule, cuts into the height of the garden door and has the most miserable little passage which serves as the line of communication from the courtyard to the garden. For a staircase in the center not to cause any obstruction it must have two flights, one on either side of the entrance door, joining in a large landing on the first floor above the door of the *salon* which would be placed between the vestibule and the garden. Such a staircase would be as magnificent as it would be comfortable and perfectly befitting the house of a prince or the palace of a king. In other houses, on which so much money should not be spent, a staircase of a single flight is sufficient; its best location is the one I have already indicated because then nothing obscures it and it obscures nothing. To make the staircase comfortable it is necessary (1) that the flights be in a straight line; (2) that the steps be wide and have a low rise; (3) that there be intermittent landings; (4) that the whole be well lit. Curved flights are always uncomfortable because the steps are deep at one end and narrow at the other so that while the foot rests precariously huge strides are needed. Narrow steps frighten and are really dangerous when going down, as is proved by those of the great altar of St. Sulpice where already more than one priest has been close to giddiness. Steep steps are tiring and take one's breath away. A long flight without a landing is just as inconvenient; this row of steps without interruption and without rest frightens when going down and tires when going up. The staircase is the part of the house which demands most light because it is here that false steps carry the greatest risk. A staircase placed in the way I have described presup-supposes a *corps de logis* of double depth, and only in a double *corps de logis* can one be comfortably housed.

The *grands appartements* must consist of at least an ante-room, a *salon de compagnie*, a bedroom and a *cabinet*. All these rooms must face the garden and be arranged *en suite*. In the front section of the double *corps de logis* must be placed the *salle à manger*, closets, dressing rooms, bath-rooms, and privies. I mention here only those things one cannot do without since they are indispensable for comfort. The *salle a manger* must be within reach of the service and the kitchen. These two rooms can only be placed conven-iently in the wings of the main building. The basements are too dark and humid and too difficult to clean to make them serve for anything other than cellar and storage rooms for wine and wood. Closets and the other *cabinets* must be within reach of the bedroom; to avoid any bad smell use should be made of privies *à l'anglaise.* The other *appartements* must all have an antechamber, a bedroom, a *cabinet*, and a closet. I do not mention the great salons, galleries, libraries, and all those rooms which are only there for the sake of magnificence. They are appropriate only for the houses of great noblemen; they should be separate from the lived-in *appartements* and this is always easy to arrange.

To make the *appartements* comfortable the following points should be observed: (1) The doors should not be too numerous, as they cause harmful drafts and make furnishing very awkward. They should be near the windows, have two leaves which when open do not extend over the thickness of the wall, and close with perfect ease. (2) The windows should be without sill and open right down to the floor because then they give infinitely better light; also one should have, when sitting, a free view over the garden; they should, like the doors, open without extending over the thickness of the wall and should close with the same accuracy and ease. (3) The fireplaces should not be opposite windows or doors, and all necessary precautions should be taken to avoid any smoke. (4) The beds should be in large alcoves because being better enclosed one keeps warmer; besides, when there is an alcove to separate the bed from the room, the furnishing of the bedroom is much easier and more graceful. Comfort would be perfect if on either side of the alcove there were a door and a passage communicating with the closets.

To be very comfortably lodged one should not have someone living above and no one should have to go upstairs. In large cities the ground is too precious to restrict all houses to a single floor. Only princes and kings can afford to be lodged with plenty of space without having to trouble about climbing stairs and without having anybody over their heads. It was very wrong not to provide this convenience in all royal houses. Does it befit a king to give up the ground floor to whomever it may be or to have a first floor in his house? Why then build a residence for him of several stories? It is not the same for private persons. The restricted size of their plots makes it necessary to lodge them over each other. However, special care must be taken, within the restriction, to arrange it so that in the upper apartment the bedroom is not over that of the lower apartment but over some other room where one does not need to fear disturbing somebody's rest.

When planning a building an architect must take care to turn the whole site to account, leaving nothing unused. If he has any idea of distribution he will greatly profit even by its irregularities and the smallest nooks will be transformed under his hand into as many advantages. In fairness to our artists: planning is a subject which they master to the highest degree. They know how to multiply the number of lodgings in small spaces and how to provide every kind of comfort for each lodging. Their skill in this kind of work has given rise to the fashion of small *appartements*. This fashion is not at all bad. All the same, it would be dangerous if it became too general and if from now on great noblemen would have a labyrinth of small cells as their lodging. Small *appartements* are suitable for a small purse, but in great houses they are always misplaced unless they are at least nearly like capricious fancies (*hors-d'oeuvres de fantaisie*).

Finally, *dégagements* contribute much to the comfort of the lodging. I shall not enlarge on the subject; it is one of those in which our architects excel. One understands the term *dégagements* to mean all rooms which serve as hidden communications from inside an apartment to the outside. These *dégagements* are necessary to avoid long roundabout routes and to have near at hand all the assistance that may come from the service hall and other servant quarters so that one is able to undress whenever one wants to and can come and go without being embarrassed and without embarrassing anyone else. It is useless to enter into great detail here; suffice it to say that *degagements* are something an architect must never neglect in the planning of an apartment.

Article III

On How to Observe *Bienséance* on Buildings

Bienséance demands that a building is neither more nor less magnificent than is appropriate to its purpose, that is to say that the decoration of buildings should not be arbitrary, but must always be in relation to the rank and quality of those who live in them and conform to the objective envisaged. To be less vague let us distinguish between public buildings and private houses.

I rank among public buildings churches, royal palaces, town halls, courts of law, hospitals and religious houses. Decorations for churches can never be dignified enough; they are the sanctuaries of the Deity. It is fitting to give them a majestic appearance equal to such a grand objective. There is never a risk of going too far. It can be said that the more magnificent our churches are the better is *bienséance* fulfilled. However, one thing has to be observed, namely that not every kind of ornament is suited to the decoration of our churches; there must be nothing profane, capricious, or indecent. There have been architects with so little judgment that they embellished the frieze of a church with all the instruments appropriate to pagan sacrifice or with monstrous figures, the products of fantasy and caprice. This means sinning openly against all rules of *bienséance.* In a church everything must be simple, virile, solemn, and serious, there must be nothing that could detract from devotion, nothing that does not sustain it and kindle its fervor. Nude figures in particular must be strictly banished from painting and sculpture. It is surprising to see them even on altars making them almost indecent and scandalous. The choir of Notre Dame is a work where the strict *bienséance* I am talking about has perhaps most scrupulously been kept. Everything in this superb decoration is noble, simple, and religious. I have only one objection: in the apse, the architecture of the church has been spoiled without reason by bulky square pillars taking the place of columns, thereby making harsh and dry something which had been rather gentle and soft.

Though magnificence in churches is necessary, there must be nothing that is superfluous. Every time I go to the Dome des Invalides the admiration aroused by this great piece of architecture, which by the way is not without fault, gives way in me to the surprise about its utter uselessness. First I come to a proper and complete church, but then I notice behind the main altar a second church, lavishly enriched with paintings, marble, sculpture, and gilding, a complete church in itself. When I ask what the use is of this great dome and everything that goes with it, nobody can give an explanation. I only see in it the fancy of a great prince who wished to create something beautiful without a clear idea of what he wanted. I can only think of one way here to save *bienséance*: that is to consecrate this useless church to the burial place of our kings. A design like this would turn this temple into a true mausoleum the shape of which it already has. In this way the ashes of our kings would be reunited with those of our great warriors who made them invincible, and this mausoleum, common to all of them, would present a monument to their greatness infinitely more awe-inspiring than the small tombs scattered here and there within the church of St. Denis. [*If this scheme which I propose is accepted it would not mean erecting a separate mausoleum. The dome itself would be the mausoleum. All it needs is to hollow out a vault in the middle of which the coffins would be placed as is done in St. Denis, and under the center of the dome the image of death* (la réprésentation mortuaire) *would be set up in a very fitting manner.*]

Royal palaces should be grand, spacious, magnificently decorated outside and richly furnished inside. Outside there must be wide avenues and courts of considerable size, inside halls, galleries, and *appartements en enfilade.* It would be tedious to revive here the distressed comments which the whole nation has been making for a long time about the chaos of hovels which completely hide the beautiful facade of the Louvre. It is to be hoped that one day the palace will be completed and that the buildings that crowd round the entrance and obstruct its approaches will then be razed to the ground. The Tuileries are in about the same position. The avenue leading to the palace is one of the worst—or rather, there is none. One must plod through a mass of small streets to arrive eventually at a small door opening into a fairly small courtyard which, like a bourgeois garden, is surrounded by plain walls. Those who built the long gallery which joins the Tuileries to the Louvre thought to have worked wonders; as a result it now happens that there are only miserable narrow thoroughfares to lead from one side of Paris to one or the other of these palaces. The Château de Versailles has beautiful avenues and very large courts, but the exterior decoration facing these courts is not at all fitting for a house in which the King of France has taken up his usual residence. Not only has this decoration nothing majestic or striking about it, it is even extremely faulty. The so-called *cour de marbre* is in every respect rather mediocre. What is this architecture encased in brick, the busts stuck against the walls, these pieces of porticoes crudely designed on the wings, these roofs uselessly laden with gilding? Let us admit that this whole arrangement is in bad taste. This courtyard is much too small for a palace of that importance. Louis XIV, who made everything on a grand scale, would never have allowed it to survive unless the respect for a house in which the King his father had lived had not prevailed in his heart over all other considerations.

To give to this part of the Chateau a really noble appearance it would need a long facade varied by pavilions of different heights and of different structure, great colonnades at the wings on an elliptical or mixtilinear plan which would serve as communication from one *corps de logis* to the other, and, through these porticoes a vista of the gardens which would give the court a surprising gaiety and an air of lightness (*dégagement*). It would need many other things which will never be. Whatever the plan and whatever the expense it will be very difficult by a simple alteration to create something beautiful and grand in the inner courtyard of the Château de Versailles. The interior is scarcely any better. Discovering eventually after a long search the staircase leading to the *appartement*, one is greatly surprised to find neither vestibule nor *salon* but two or three small rooms leading to an anteroom entered from a corner and lit by a lucarne; nevertheless, that is the King's anteroom. From there one proceeds to the bedroom and the *cabinet*. Here the enfilade is again interrupted and the *appartement* continues at right angles along one of the wings. Having passed through it all, one returns saying: I do not think much of the way in which the greatest king in the world is lodged. You then inquire for that famous gallery of which there is so much talk. If you want to take the shortest way, somebody opens for you one half of a mirror, and there you are in the gallery without knowing how you got there. If, however, you want to be shown there by the *belle entrée*, you must go down again and cross the courtyard; then you are led to another staircase, at a place as unpredictable as the previous one. You ascend and there you are—not in a vestibule but in the middle of the *grand appartement*. From there you pass several rooms of various sizes and at last arrive in the magnificent salon that is the true entrance to the gallery.

93

[*Some time ago the staircase* des Ambassadeurs *was demolished. So what happens? This whole part of the Chateau
is now without a staircase and during ceremonies the Court
has no other place to descend to the chapel than by the two
breakneck passages at the side of the King's Gallery. Where
now to place a convenient staircase? Here is an idea that has
occurred to me. One could construct on the outside a staircase* en fer-à-cheval *or of two flights on which to go up from
the small courtyard to the* salon d'Hercule; *its three windows
facing the courtyard would be converted into three doors to
open onto this staircase. On ground level between the two
flights a passage for carriages would have to be left. I propose
a slight remedy for a great ill but, although this staircase
would be placed where it certainly should not be, it would
provide a convenience which, after all, one cannot do
without.*]

The Château de Versailles certainly contains things of very
great beauty, but there are few buildings that are so full of
faults. Only its spaciousness and the abundance of valuable
objects of every style make it worthy of a great prince. The
many masterpieces with which this stately palace is filled
will at all times and rightly excite the curiosity of amateurs.
Nowhere in the world does one find so many marvels to
admire. How unfortunate that for connoisseurs admiration is
not complete and that the great beauty displayed in the
architecture is disfigured for them by great blemishes. Nothing proves better that imperfection is the fate of things made
by men.

Up to a certain degree magnificence is proper for municipal buildings, courts of law, houses around a public square,
and other public buildings of a similar kind. I will say
nothing of the town hall of Paris; the resolution, passed
recently, to build a new one proves that the imperfection of
the old one is fully perceived. The so-called *Palais* is spacious
but otherwise nothing, outside or inside, comes up to the

lofty idea one must have of a place which on every account is worthy of respect. Our squares all lack that certain air of grandeur which would suit them so well. The Place Royale, the most spacious of all, could be beautiful if the iron grille round the center, resembling a garden enclosure, were broken up, if the squat porticoes which run all the way round and are worth less than the worst cloisters of a monastery were bricked up, if the great pavilions which conceal the two main entrances were demolished, if the four corners were opened up by great streets—with all this done it would look like a square. As it is, it can only be taken for a courtyard the center of which has been turned into a garden. The Place des Victoires, although the smallest, is however the most beautiful because of the many wide streets leading to it. The Place Louis le Grand is generally admired for its strict symmetry and rich architecture. Close attention to the principles I have established in the first chapter would reveal many reprehensible flaws in the architecture of the buildings surrounding this square. Furthermore, the decoration of these buildings is without variation of any kind and the square itself is like an isolated courtyard to which no street leads directly and which is so well enclosed on all sides that, standing in the center, one would be led to believe that there is no way of getting out. For a square to be beautiful it should be a communal center from which people can make their way into different quarters and where, coming from different quarters they can gather together; for that reason several streets must lead to it like the roads of a forest to a *carrefour*. Porticoes are the right decoration for squares and if joined to these there are buildings of different height and shape, the decoration will be perfect. Symmetry is necessary but also a certain disorder that varies and heightens the spectacle. Squares can be adorned by fountains and statues. We really do not have a beautiful fountain at all. Those who write guidebooks have made up their minds that the fountain of the Saints Innocents is to rank among the marvels of this capital. The chisel that cut out the sculptures can, in fact, be praised, but can anybody say that a square tower with windows in between two pilasters is the right idea for a fountain? Will I be referred to the rue de Grenelle so that I shall see something better? I admit that there I find beautiful statues and fine marble. I think I see a retable of an altar and am much surprised to learn from the water running at the bottom that it is a fountain. The rare talent and the noble ambition of the famous Bouchardon cannot be praised enough; if in sculpture we are today superior to other nations, we are mainly indebted for this to the new Phidias. With his genius he could have made a masterpiece of this fountain of which I condemn the idea and admire the execution. He should have been given a more convenient and more advantageous place; besides, not having been free to conceive and invent as he pleased it was almost inevitable that he should give way to a false conception. In this respect the Italians greatly surpass us. One must go to Rome to develop a taste for beautiful fountains. There they are in great numbers and although they differ from each other, they all have a *je ne sais quoi* of a true and natural style which is enchanting. Is there anything as delightful, as noble and as characteristic as the fountain of the Piazza Navona? Here is a model we have not yet come anywhere near.

Statues are the most common ornament of our squares. It is a most reasonable and well conceived idea to prefer squares to any other location for erecting a monument to the immortal memory of our good kings, but it would be absurd to establish as a principle that every statute must have a square. In our days we have seen thoughtless people make the rash proposal to pull down eight or nine hundred houses to make room for a statue of Louis XV. The King in his usual noble way of thinking opposed so cruel a devastation of his capital and preferred having his statue less well placed to dislodging ten thousand citizens by force.[1] Accordingly the plan was changed, but the idea of a square has not been dropped. It is still thought that the king's statue cannot do without this costly appendage. There is some talk, I am told, of laying out a square on the large plot of land between the Pont tournant and the Champs Elysées. I do not doubt that with a great deal of expense one could succeed in creating something beautiful, but it will always be true to say that it is a square in the middle of fields and this thought is enough to hold this project up to ridicule. And why! Does a statue demand a square on principle? Is the position of Henry IV's statue on the Pont Neuf not a hundred times better than that of all the others? What could be the drawback of assigning this same Pont Neuf as a place to bring together the various statues of our kings which the love of the people would wish to see erected? It seems to me that without much expense one could set up on this bridge massive socles at regular intervals on which many statues could be mounted. With such embellishment it would be made into the most beautiful bridge in the world, very favorably situated in the center and at the most prominent place in the town. If one persists in demanding a square for every statue that is erected it would need one of two things, either depopulate Paris or enlarge it every time a statue is set up. The Romans were wiser than we. They have erected more statues than we ever will. Having done everything to make them perfect, they then placed them wherever they could without embarrassing or upsetting anybody.

With an increasing number of statues it would be reasonable to vary the design. There are already three equestrian statues—that is enough uniformity. Only the Place des Victoires presents a statue of a different type. It is desirable that from now on our sculptors produce new ideas. By using groups it would be easy for them to avoid too frequent repetition of the same design; then they could give these

[1]In 2nd ed. changed to: thirty thousand (translator's note).

97

monuments an expressive and imaginative liveliness which nearly all of them lack. I do not know if the current way of dressing statues is the best and most fitting one. Why mislead posterity? Why disguise our heroes under a dress that was not customary in our times? If the Romans had had this bizarre idea we would be very annoyed with them. To suppress or change what could in the eyes of future centuries characterize our nation and our century is acting dishonestly. [*This fault was not committed with the statue of Henry IV; although not dressed in Roman fashion it is not less worthy of admiration.*]

Hospitals must be built solidly but must be simple. In no other building would opulence be more contrary to *bien-séance*. Buildings intended to house the poor must retain something of poverty. The new hospital of the Enfants-trouves looks more like a palace than a hospital. So much splendor indicates either a superabundant endowment or little economy in the administration. It is, therefore, a very misplaced splendor. Nothing is more elegant than the chapel of this hospital the decoration of which is a little masterpiece. A truly fortunate idea is executed in a manner that is as ingenuous as its conception is noble, but, once again, too much beauty in one building ceases to arouse charity because curiosity finds too much to indulge in. The poor people must be housed like poor people—with much cleanliness and comfort, but with no ostentation!

I say as much of seminaries or regular and secular houses. Facades of this class of buildings must always show all the simplicity befitting the status of the people living there. Anything which indicates lavish expenditure, anything which is purely ornamental must be excluded. The public, amateur of *bienséance*, always sees with regret these splendid facades adorning houses in which only contempt of the world and the spirit of retreat and repentance should reign.

As to private houses, *bienséance* requires that their decoration be commensurate with the rank and wealth of the owners. I have nothing in particular to observe in this respect except that it would be desirable if everybody recognized his own merit so well that one did not see people who, with only opulence to speak for them, equal and even surpass the first lords and greatest noblemen of the kingdom through the exterior and interior magnificence of their houses. I admit that architects are not always free to follow strictly the *bienséances* of which I have spoken. The vainglory of private clients prescribes to them laws to which they are forced to submit. Nevertheless, it usually depends on the architect who has produced the design to give it more or less simplicity according to the *bienséance* required by the subject. When he is consulted, he must only propose what is fitting. If he has his reputation at heart he will not look for dazzling designs to flatter the vanity of people to whom splendor is not at all fitting and who themselves are often too inclined to go beyond the limits. An architect, knowing well what is fitting to each person, will elaborate or restrain his plans according to his judgment, never forgetting this true principle that a beautiful building is not one that has any kind of beauty (*beauté arbitraire*), but one that, considering the circumstances, has all the beauty that is befitting and nothing beyond.

Chapter IV

On the Style in Which to Build Churches

Of all buildings churches give architects the best opportunity to display the marvels of their art. Since our churches are meant to receive into their midst a multitude bringing with them the religious image of the God they are going to worship, these churches give the architect scope for working on a large scale and do not in any way restrict the nobility of his concepts. It is surprising that, whereas in any other class there are buildings worthy of admiration, so few of our churches deserve our enlightened interest. For myself, I am convinced that until now we have not developed the right style for this class of building. Our Gothic churches are still the most acceptable. A mass of grotesque ornaments spoils them, and yet, we are awed by a certain air of greatness and majesty. Here we find ease and gracefulness; they only lack simplicity and naturalness. We have rightly renounced the follies of Gothic (*l'architecture moderne*) and have returned to the antique, but it seems we have lost good taste on the way. Moving away from the Gothic architects (*Modernes*) we deserted gracefulness; turning towards the antique we encountered clumsiness; this happened because we have gone half the way. We have halted between two styles, and the result is a new kind of architecture that is only half antique and may make us regret having abandoned Gothic architecture altogether. A simple critical comparison will make this clear.

I enter Notre Dame, the most eminent of our Gothic buildings in Paris, though not by far as beautiful as certain others in the provinces which everybody admires. Nevertheless, at first glance my attention is captured, my imagination is struck by the size, the height and the unobstructed view (*dégagement*) of the vast nave; for some moments I am lost in the amazement that the grand effect of the whole stirs in me. Recovering from the first astonishment and taking note now of the details, I find innumerable absurdities, but I lay the blame for them on the misfortunes of the time. For all that I am still full of admiration when after my thorough and critical examination I return to the middle of the nave and the impression which remains with me makes me say: "How many faults, but how grand!" From there I go to St. Sulpice, the most eminent of all churches we have built in the antique style. It neither strikes me nor impresses me; I find the building to be far below its reputation. I see nothing but thick masses. There are heavy arches set between heavy pilasters of a very heavy and coarse Corinthian Order, and over the whole lies a heavy vault the weight of which makes you fear that the heavy supports may be insufficient. What shall I say of the screen (*jube*) which conceals the main entrance to the church? It is a pretty piece of architecture, but is as little in its proper place as a small house is inside a large one. What shall I say of the main facade? It is an excellent idea which, however, has not come off. M. Servandoni almost reached perfection, yet stopped just short of it. In order to make something out of the facade, the columns should not have been coupled in depth but lengthwise; the enormous Doric cornice of the main entablature, difficult to protect from damage caused by weather, should have been suppressed and the free-standing columns of the first Order repeated in the second, an arrangement that would at least have saved the building from its extreme coarseness. The towers should have been separated from the central part of the facade and been given a less dry and heavy form. I shall not elaborate observations on a building which will always be deplored by connoisseurs and, while immortalizing the devotion and good intentions of the well-known M. Languet, will prove to posterity that our century is not at all the century of good architecture.

Nearly all our churches are in the same style. They always have pilasters, arches and a vault and are more or less heavy. They all lack real grace and majesty. I, therefore, conclude that in this class we have not yet achieved the right way of building. I shall set out here my ideas, the result of much thinking and long study. My conception seems to me much better than what is being done. Connoisseurs and the masters of the art shall be my judges.

With regard to churches we have so far done nothing but copy the Gothic buildings of our ancestors. Like them we make naves, aisles, crossings, choirs and round apses; we put arcades where they put them and arrange the windows as they did, only not as well. The only difference is that our modern churches give at least an imperfect idea of true architecture and that in Gothic churches anything in this style is defective. We criticize the height of their vaults. Yet surely this excessive height contributes greatly to the majestic appearance of the building. It is true that as long as we follow the rules which up till now we have set ourselves we cannot give our churches the same elevation. Consequently they would seem much too low and can, therefore, never make a satisfying impression.

I have tried to find if, in building our churches in the good style of classical architecture, there is not a way to give them an elevation and a lightness equal to those of our beautiful Gothic churches. After much thought it seemed to me that not only would it be possible but that it would be much easier for us to succeed in this with the architecture of the Greeks than with all the fretwork of Gothic architecture. By using free-standing columns we will achieve lightness and by setting two Orders one above the other we will reach the required height.

Here is how I should like my idea to be carried out. Let us choose the most common form, that of the Latin cross. I place all around the nave, transept and choir the first Order of isolated columns standing on low socles; they are coupled like those of the portico of the Louvre in order to give more width to the intercolumniations. On these columns I place a straight architrave terminated by an ogee of moderate projection and erect over this a second Order, consisting, like the first one, of free-standing and coupled columns. This second Order has its complete straight entablature and, directly over it without any sort of attic, I erect a plain barrel vault without transverse ribs. Then, around the nave, crossing, and choir I arrange columned aisles which form a true peristyle and are covered by flat ceilings placed on the architraves of the first Order. Beyond this peristyle I arrange chapels with an opening as wide as the intercolumniations. The form of these chapels is a perfect square with four columns in the corners supporting an architrave and flat ceiling. Each chapel has two open and two closed sides. The two which are open are those of the entrances with only a simple grille, and those opposite completely glazed. The two other sides, sepa-rating one chapel from the other, are taken up one by the altar, the other by a correspondingly large piece of painting or sculpture. Finally, I have the great vault supported by flying buttresses, based on the walls separating one chapel from the other and abutting on a point just above the capitals of the second Order.

This then is my idea and here are the advantages: (1) A building like this is entirely natural and true; everything is reduced to simple rules and executed according to great principles: no arcades, no pilasters, no pedestals, nothing awkward or constrained. (2) The whole building is extremely elegant and delicate; the plain wall is nowhere to be seen, therefore, nothing is superfluous, nothing is bulky, nothing is offensive. (3) The windows are placed in the most suitable and most advantageous position. All intercolumniations are glazed, above and below. There are no more plain lunettes cutting into the vault as in ordinary churches, but ordinary large windows. (4) The two Orders placed one above the other bring nave, crossing and choir to the height that produces the majestic effect, a height which is in no way irregular and does not require columns of an exorbitant scale. (5) The vault, although a barrel vault, loses all heaviness through this height, especially since it has no transverse ribs which would appear to weigh down heavily. (6) Splendor and magnificence could easily be added to the *dégagement*, simplicity, elegance and dignity of such a building. All it needs is for the different parts to be decorated in good taste. Even the vault, being quite plain, could serve as ground on which to display a grand design of painting and sculpture. It is, therefore, clear that this kind of building would in every respect be preferable to the ordinary one. Let us consider the drawbacks and difficulties which may stand in its way.

It is no longer a question of arguing about the alleged impossibility of building straight entablatures; I have already replied that one only needs to study the straight line of the bays of the Chapel of Versailles or of the entablature of the portico of the Louvre; these two examples dissolve the difficulty completely.

[*The author of the* Examen *declares that the example of the Chapel of Versailles does not prove anything. "Open your eyes," he says, "and see that these columns rest on a substructure of arcades on the ground floor which convinces the eye of their solidity." But in return I ask him: "If this ground floor which is the greatest fault of the chapel were concealed through laying a floor at the level of the colonnade so that one walked on the same level from the King's Gallery to the organ, would the chapel lose its solidity?" Certainly not. Well then, if such a substructure is considered necessary underneath the columns all one has to do is to construct one in the basement under the floor of the church.*]

It will perhaps be said that mere columns could not support a vault as large as that of a church. I reply that nothing is more illusory than this difficulty. The load will not be too heavy for the columns if the vault is only of medium thickness, and why should great thickness be necessary? The thrust of the vault will be sufficiently resisted by the flying buttresses, as it is in Gothic churches. Therefore, I cannot see what is impossible about it. Several churches already exist where the main vault is upheld only by columns. In Notre Dame especially everything is carried on simple columns which form the peristyle of the aisles. [*These columns are, it is true, very badly proportioned, but this fault of proportion which hurts the eye does not increase their solidity. Besides, there are so many other examples of Gothic buildings which as support have only columns of a height that is excessive in relation to their diameter. It is true that the eye is frightened because it does not judge the columns to have sufficient solidity, but has it ever made the same judgment about columns made according to the right proportions? The eye looks with admiration and without being hurt at the columns on the portico of the church of the Sorbonne facing the courtyard. One may increase the module of the columns as much as one wants; the effect, since the proportion does not vary, will always be the same.*]

To the objection that it is impossible for the barrel vault to have to rest directly on the straight entablature of the second Order I reply that the vault would not rest at all on this entablature but could be held up at the intercolumniations by an extremely shallow arch leaving a small void which could easily be filled in later. To the further objection that a construction like that costs too much, I reply that it would cost less in material and more in labor. The workmen must have more skill and precision; it is for them to acquire both these qualities. A gifted and ambitious architect can easily overcome this difficulty by supervising the work with scrupulous care and by marking out accurately the job for the workmen who always carry out faithfully what is demanded of them. Besides, when the intention is to create something beautiful, a small rise in cost should not be a consideration. If our ancestors had thought about cost, the churches of Amiens, Bourges and Rheims would never have come into existence. The great aim in art is to create something perfect and to spare no pains to succeed.

[*I have noticed with satisfaction that everybody was struck by the beauty of the plan I have just outlined. Its simplicity, naturalness and elegance made many people wish to see it executed. However, there is a great difficulty. Not that it would be impossible to give sufficient solidity to a building constructed in this way. I have shown in my* avertissement[1] *that the misgivings of the architects are baseless in this respect. Two almost insurmountable obstacles are opposed to the fulfillment of our wishes: the prejudice of the mind and the habit of the hand. It is beyond human strength, more than anything else, to change the ideas and opinions of men who believe they were created to dominate others and who suppose that the purpose of proposing new practices to them*

[1]See p. 156ff. (translator's note).

is to dominate them. The rule of reason alone could not prevail at the first attempt over the resistance massed against it by prejudice of education, displeasure about being forced to retrace one's steps, and even shame for having to submit to new studies when one believed one's complete store of enlightened knowledge had already been acquired. The result of all this in the mind is a sad prejudice to which pride has contributed most and which confronts all reasoning with an arrogant obstinacy that simple ignorance would not have. It is, therefore, first a question of overcoming the interest which the masters may have in not allowing a new method to find favor. It is obvious that victory cannot be obtained without enduring great fights. Instead of giving up the scheme of false defense for the love of truth, they will cause difficulties over difficulties and will dispute the ground step by step so as never to surrender. It needs much time and reflection to extinguish this first heat of opposition so that reason can regain its right. It needs even greater honesty and nobility of heart to rise above a prejudice unfortunately so common although so pernicious and blind.

Even when the prejudice of the mind begins to disappear, it would still remain for the habit of the hand to be reformed. This second obstacle will always slow down success. It is not at all easy to make the workmen execute things which they have never done. Their imaginations rebel, their ideas are confounded and their hands refuse to work. It needs an ardor and a patience, of which few people are capable, to drag the workman away from the ordinary routine and to lead him on a route which is completely unknown to him. One must endure from him much grumbling, engage with him in many quarrels, smoothe over many of his aversions. Only by overcoming all these difficulties have the architects of the fifteenth century brought about the revolution that gave the deathblow to Gothic architecture and restored over its debris the antique systems (ordonnances). *To break free from the chain of prejudice and habit it needs a Brunelleschi[1] or a Bramante.*

The ordinary custom with us is to end churches in a round apse. The question here to be examined first is whether it is advisable to retain this custom, how far it serves some useful need and even whether it accords with good rules. A round apse is pleasing to the eyes of many—but what is its purpose, what does it signify? With a rectangular plan, such as that of our churches, it is very difficult to conceal all the awkward effects caused by the mixture of curved and straight lines. These are as follows: (1) The region where the curved line of the apse connects with the straight line of the chancel always jars. If this point of juncture corresponds exactly to the center of the column, as it should do, half of the column would always be at *porte-à-faux*. (2) The aisles necessarily turn around the apse on a circular plan. In consequence one cannot see distinctly from one end of the aisle to the other since the view finishes in an ambiguous way at the far end where the circular plan begins. (3) In the ambulatory the ceilings of the aisles are not square anymore. They take on a most irregular shape: two sides are straight but not parallel while the other two are sections of concentric circles. I have already said that in architecture these irregular shapes must under any circumstances be avoided. (4) The intercolumniations in the ambulatory can no longer be equally spaced and this is the worst fault. Instead, if everything ends in rectangular lines one does not need to fear these awkward effects.

I do not see that round apses have any advantage which would entitle one to disregard the inconvenience that could result. It is claimed that their shape is pleasing and that this way of ending a church has a lively grace which has led

[1]Brunelleschi is the first of the Moderns who, by studying the ancient monuments and measuring their parts, revived the idea of the Doric, Ionic and Corinthian Orders.

architects to use it everywhere. I admit that, generally speaking, round plans are somewhat less dry and more elegant than plans on straight lines and that round forms are by themselves preferable to angular ones, but the main thing is to use them well. When they involve inconvenience and bring confusion and disorder into the composition, then their use cannot be reprehensible. It is the same as in rhetoric where phrases, when misplaced, render the discourse faulty.

I have considered for a long time whether it would not be possible to retain these pleasing round apses without falling into the awkward effects I have just been talking about. Here is what has occurred to me. A very simple way would be not to have the aisles turn around the apse but to terminate them in a rectangular form where the round apse begins; in this way there would be only a single circular plan and all further concentric circles eliminated, an arrangement that was common in our ancient churches. This universal custom of old has an advantage, namely that the round apse can be glazed from top to bottom, which would give it a lightness and brilliancy without comparison. A second way of which I have not seen any examples would be to let the peristyles of the aisles turn round the nave, crossing and apse, everywhere in straight lines and right angles while the inner sanctuary would end in a sort of demi-dome with its own columns differing from those of the peristyle. By this scheme most of the drawbacks of the round apse would be avoided, but some others would arise which are of some consequence: (1) There would be in this round apse an altogether disagreeable confusion of columns. (2) The circular architraves of the demi-dome would not at all fit in with the rectangular architraves of the aisles. (3) There would remain between the demi-dome and the peristyles of the aisles on both sides an open space in the very irregular shape of a right-angled triangle of which the hypotenuse would be curved.

All these considerations make me conclude that it would be

best to do without the round apse and let the choir end in
straight lines. But in case one is absolutely unwilling to give
up the round apse, I believe it to be in good taste and a sign
of fine feeling (*bonne entente*) for the plan to end not only
the choir but also the two arms of the transept in round apses
as has been done in the church of St. Peter's in Rome.

I have said before that the use of domes cannot be condemned strongly enough; the form in which they have been
executed until now is contrary to all rules of good architecture. If one wants to give the vault a greater height in the
center of the crossing than elsewhere, one can erect in the
form of a dome a kind of baldachino which, delicately
designed, can have something in common with the idea of a
vault. Consequently there are no columns, nothing at all that
needs to be supported from the foundations upwards. An
architect will easily understand the reasons which have led
me to the conclusions. Taking up the idea which I have
presented to him he will with genius and talent design a vault
that will have all the advantages of a dome without its
drawbacks. [*One could, for instance, erect a saucer dome*
(calotte) *in the shape of a tiara or of a paraboloid. One could
decorate it in such a way that it would appear to be
openwork imitating in some manner the skillful device* (arti-
fice) *of Gothic rose windows with their light tracery and
merely outline the contours with less harshness and more
naturalness and grace. This dome, shaped as a* calotte *inside,
could be given a different form outside much nearer to that
of ordinary domes. It would not be impossible to join harmoniously two forms so contradictory in appearance. I admit
that it will cost much study and thought, but did it not cost
much to the first inventor of domes? I ask our architects
sometimes to depart from the ordinary route. Their real fame
rests on their inventions. Only by making things which have
not yet been made will they give proof of their genius. If
those in whose footsteps they follow had always wanted to*

walk in those of their predecessors, where would architecture be today?]

Having constructed the interior of the church it only remains to settle the arrangement and decoration of altars. I am not at all of the opinion of those who want to have the main altar placed in the center of the crossing directly under the dome which as in St. Peter's in Rome would serve as a baldachino. I admit that this place is the most advantageous of all since this is the point where all parts of the building meet and which is in the sight of the greatest number of people. The following reasons, however, have led me not to put the altar in this the most apparent place:

1. It is very difficult to think of a design for an altar which can give, even if only slightly, an impression of majesty when placed in the center of a void as large as that which occurs in the middle of the crossing. Look at the main altar of St. Sulpice, notice how insignificant it appears at first sight although its size is so enormous that only a rather narrow space remains to walk around it. This would be much worse if, instead of placing it at the entrance of the choir, it had been moved forward into the center of the crossing. At St. Peter's in Rome this fault has been corrected by erecting a tall and magnificent baldachino over the main altar. But to imitate this scheme means putting one baldachino underneath another and one small house inside a large one.

2. An altar placed in this way cuts the church in two and prevents the view from ranging freely from one end of the church to the other which greatly reduces the spectator's pleasure.

3. This position hides from the people the spectacle of the ceremonies which are conducted in the choir during celebration of Divine Service and makes it impossible for those who are in the choir to see anything of what takes place at the altar. These seem to me sufficient reasons for concluding that the center of the crossing is not the most suitable place for the

principal altar. My opinion is that it should always be placed at the far end of the choir provided that all ambos are removed which in nearly all our cathedrals block the entrance to the choir making it impenetrable in every respect.

Therefore, I would enclose the choir along its whole circumference with a simple grille which would in no way obstruct the view. The stalls would be situated in the forepart of the choir to the right and to the left; there would be no lectern of any kind in the center to obscure the view of the sanctuary. This sanctuary would be raised a few steps above the pavement of the choir. In the middle of the sanctuary I would build a large platform, several steps high and free on all sides so that one can easily move around it. The altar would be placed in the center of this platform. It is evident that such a position has all the advantages one can wish for. The altar is seen by everybody and, closely surrounded by the peristyle of the sanctuary, its whole composition will have an air of magnificence and grandeur. It is easy to decorate it in a style which is at the same time simple and majestic. Here is roughly how the decoration should be.

A tomb, well designed and unaffected in its appearance, is the most fitting form for an altar because it recalls the ancient custom of the Church to celebrate the Holy Mysteries over the tomb of the martyrs. Two simple tiers above the tomb with an urn in the middle serving as tabernacle and two worshipping angels at each end are all that is necessary. Anything added to it would be superfluous and fanciful. In this respect the altar of Notre Dame can serve as model. The parts close to the altar can be embellished and can thus contribute to the decoration of the altar itself. In the inter-columniations surrounding the sanctuary one can place groups in marble or bronze which relate to the particular subject to which this altar is dedicated and, in the middle, at the height of the architrave between the two Orders, a *gloire*

112

with several groups of angels flying in the open space around the core of rays and the name of God in the triangle. The whole architecture of the sanctuary can be in marble and all the sculpture be gilded. This decoration can be completed by a large painting on the vault which relates to the objects represented below so that in the end the decision of the whole is unique and true.

An altar arranged in the way I have just indicated would be of perfect beauty and present a magnificent sight. Divine Service would be conducted here with great ease and the ceremonies would be seen by all the people. Furthermore, there would be no false or sham ornaments, everything would conform to the simplicity and true taste of *la bonne architecture.* Therefore, I do not hesitate to prefer it to all these ridiculous retables which until now made up the decoration of our altars, retables overloaded with misplaced columns, niches, pediments, cartouches, statues and pedestals scattered here and there without order and design, retables which, far from forming a whole with the architecture of the church, only serve to obscure, interrupt and disfigure it and to create confusion and disorder.

I would not wish the ends of the transepts to serve exclusively as vestibule to a great portal. These two places are too valuable to be used to no better advantage. I would place there two principal altars, not so richly decorated but in the same style as the one I have just proposed for the main altar. Should one object that doors are necessary in these two places to facilitate the exit of the crowds on holy days, I reply that one could easily find the way back to these doors along the aisles which lead round the ends of the transepts.

The altars of the chapels should all have a certain uniformity in design which does not exclude a variation in ideas. I have nothing in particular to recommend to our artists; I leave free play to their inventiveness provided they do not take it into their heads to introduce columns and entablatures but keep it all sober, unpretentious and religious.

Of the interior of the church only the end of the nave towards the main entrance remains to be dealt with. Ordinarily this place is reserved for the organ chest and that is really the best solution. I do not, however, approve of the almost universal custom of constructing a great tribune for this purpose. Since this tribune is essentially not a part of or is rather completely foreign to the architecture of the church it can only pervert and mar the whole architectural order (*ordonnance*). It would be much better to mount a shell made of wood over the interior door, held up firmly by angels, and to place on this base the organ chest which, giving the impression of being carried in midair, would look very graceful. This idea which I only indicate can easily be developed, corrected and improved. [*If the size of the organ chest requires it one can also have the lower portico run as an aisle in front of the main door; one will then have on top a tribune large enough to place the organ chest in the back of it, the choir organ in front and the bellows here and there.*]

I now come to the exterior of the church. What most disfigures the outside of our churches are the buttresses and flying buttresses. Since they cannot be completely suppressed, they must be obscured so that they are not visible from anywhere. Care has been taken of this when building the church of St. Peter's in Rome. From whatever side the building is seen the device is so well hidden that nothing appears that indicates the pressure of the vaults. Let us imitate this idea, which always seemed to be extremely sensible and which we ourselves have not yet thought of. Instead of ending the outer walls of the chapels at the level from which the buttresses or flying buttresses rise, let us raise them by one more story; all flying buttresses will then be hidden from view. But in order that the light in the nave be not too dim, the upper story should be opened up by as many windows as there are in the one below. It is true that this would mean an increase in labor and cost, but I have already said that this is not a consideration to stop us from doing something well. The decoration of these outer walls must be very simple. I would not employ an Order in this place because it seems to me absurd to make the outside and inside decoration equally rich; besides, it is difficult to execute an Order correctly on the outside without making the constraints inside even more stringent. I should want only a socle at the base, a plinth which separates the two stories, a cornice at the top surmounted by a balustrade and glazed windows like those below. It seems to me that no more is needed and that nevertheless this simple decoration would have all the befitting propriety.

The exception is the main entrance front and the two small portals should these be wanted at the two ends of the transept. *Bienséance* demands that the entrance to the house of God is decorated in a way to inspire in advance respect for Divinity; the faithful, approaching the church, must be struck with awe (*sainte terreur*) at the mere sight of such a venerable place. It has always been the custom to give church facades a rich decor. It even seems that in the past the inclination was to increase the number of ornaments excessively. This profusion is noticeable on all facades of Gothic churches; I am far from proposing this as a model. It is ridiculous to give the ornaments on the outside a brilliance and splendor that surpasses those of the inside. There must be gradation in everything. The exterior decoration gives at best a foretaste of the beautiful interior and prepares for it so that when passing from the outside into the interior our admiration, far from being arrested or weakened, deepens. This principle is rooted in truth and nature; let our ideas and designs strictly conform to it.

The best way of decorating the main front of a church is to build a portico across the whole width of the nave and aisles up to the same height as that of the aisles inside. This portico is to be covered by a flat roof at the far end of which rises the second Order, like the one inside, with an entablature crowned by a balustrade. Should the roof of the church be higher than the second Order, one must erect a third one, only as wide as the nave, and could terminate it by a pediment thereby observing all the rules I laid down before when dealing with the Orders on multistoried buildings. This main front should be flanked by two projecting towers (*en avant-corps*).

Our forefathers excelled in the building of towers. They caught the feeling for it marvelously and carried the skill far. They found the secret of combining elegant forms with delicate and fine workmanship and, avoiding both the too slender and the massive, achieved the degree of accuracy that results in the true beauty of this class of buildings. Nothing can be compared to the tower of Strasbourg Cathedral. This superb pyramid is a masterpiece ravishing in its prodigious height, its accurate diminution, agreeable form, the precision of its proportions and the unique delicacy of its detail. I do not believe that any architect has ever produced anything as boldly conceived, as happily thought out, as correctly executed. There is more art and genius in this one building than in all the great marvels we see elsewhere.

I do not dare to propose to our artists that by trying to imitate they give us something similar; they would soon despair of success. They have neither the imagination lively enough to dare nor the hand sure enough to execute such great things. I only beg them to reflect upon the enormous difference that exists between the towers they build and the ancient towers. Nearly all of these have boldness, grace and something that is grand and stately, while ours are just heavy with a good deal of harshness without elegance, originality or taste. This decline in such an important part of architecture is quite humiliating. Let us try to put it right if possible.

Three things make the beauty of the ancient towers: their great height, their pyramidal form and their fine and delicate workmanship. Our new towers have none of these qualities; that is why they cannot stand the comparison with those that were built before. The main facade of St. Sulpice is flanked by two towers. The expenditure has been enormous, but with what poor results! Nothing is as dry, as miserable, as disagreeable as these two towers. The lack of height is very noticeable. Far from forming a pyramid, each tower consists of two square buildings one on top of the other surmounted by a kind of dome, meager in its proportions and crude in its shape. There is not even a shadow of finesse in the workmanship. Every detail is massive, harsh, awkward, and flat. Can one be surprised that even common people disapprove of these towers and seem to be shocked by their bad effect?

It is not at all impossible to do better. Very beautiful towers can be built by using the Orders. For that it is necessary that (1) the different stories are recessed; this produces the pyramidal diminution; (2) one eliminates in the lower stories all parts of the entablature which by protruding cut up the work and convey the idea, not of a whole, but of disjointed pieces without coherence; (3) from the second story the tower ceases to be square and becomes octagonal or at least takes on any other form one wants which comes nearer to the round and keeps away from the harsh dryness of the square; (4) only free-standing columns are used so that the tower is like openwork which makes it look light and delicate. The Cavaliere Bernini, when commissioned to erect two towers over the main facade of St. Peter's in Rome, invented a design in the manner I have just described. Had it been possible to build these two towers, they would have been of an accomplished beauty. One can consult and study the design as a model.

It may perhaps be even easier to build beautiful towers without any Order and give free rein to any bold and even capricious inspiration. If there is a type of building where it is permitted to stray from the common route and follow freely the fire of one's own imagination, then it is the tower. Who prevents one from using any unique feature a fortunate genius is able to devise? Providing nothing violates common sense and reason, provided the bulk is commensurate to the height and diminution is neither too great nor too small, then the work can be embellished as much as is desired. The freer and lighter the design of the tower, the more will it appear to have been created at one stroke and the more agreeable it will be. The idea of beautiful Gothic towers, like that of Strasbourg, is excellent; only the ornaments are badly designed. Let us take up this idea and replace these grotesque (*baroques*) ornaments with true, natural, original and, without ever overstepping the limits, even with bizarre forms and we shall create something beautiful, surprising and prodigious.

Having outlined the general idea of a church facade I should mention that, if statues are wanted, they should only be placed in the intercolumniations of the portico standing on pedestals. It would even be perfectly right as a decoration to place in all intercolumniations which are not in front of the door groups of statues expressing respect, silence, recollection, faith and other sentiments which should be in the heart of the faithful coming to worship the Lord in his Holy House. Instead of groups one could represent the same subjects by bas-reliefs which would fill the void of the intercolumniations and in this way would hide the bare wall completely. In the intercolumniations of the upper stories there should be only windows, real or blind. At most, one can place groups of statues on the acroterias which intersect the upper balustrade of the portico. At the upper story with its pediment one must avoid placing on its inclines figures casually posing, as is so often done. Nothing is more absurd and unnatural than statues on roofs. It would be good to place as a final ornament at the apex of the pediment two angels who, flying on clouds, carry the cross, the crowning piece of the whole facade.

I ought to mention also that the designs for facades can be varied ad infinitum. One can erect a true dome, circular or oval in shape, in the middle to serve as main entrance and two circular porticoes at each side to provide communication between this dome in the center and the two towers at either end. Such a design would be of great magnificence. Artists will, no doubt, think of other designs, everyone according to his talent and taste. I cannot urge them too strongly to develop their own ideas, to mistrust everything that is only routine, to invent and to offer something new.

So far I have only talked of churches in the conventional form of the Latin cross. However, within the same architectural system (*ordonnance*) one can give churches all forms imaginable; it is even good not to make them all according to the same plan. All geometrical figures, from the triangle to the circle, can serve to vary continuously the composition of these buildings. No doubt it would be very pleasant if in a town like Paris there were no single church resembling another, and if each had something special in form worthy of attracting the attention of the *curieux* and of engaging the interest of the connoisseurs.

[*The author of the* Examen *finds it very wrong that I permit variation in the plan of our churches by introducing all geometrical shapes from the triangle to the circle. He believes that this diversity will create monstrous confusion and become an inexhaustible source of follies and ridiculous constructions. "What an agreeable sight," he exclaims, "a church erected over the plan of an equilateral triangle!" I am quite mortified to see that all objections raised by this critic reveal a genius to whom inventions are troublesome and incapable of bringing forth anything new. No doubt at all, it is easy to erect over the plan of an equilateral triangle a*

*church which will look most attractive. This is how I would
set about it. I inscribe in the triangle a circle that gives me
the outline of a dome which I let rise from the ground. At the
three angles I construct three rotundas which give me three
sanctuaries where I place three altars. In the center of each of
the three facades I make an opening for a door which
produces three entrances each having an altar facing them.
The dome has two great stories of architectural design, the
rest with the three rotundas only one. I maintain that such an
ordonnance would be equally beautiful, outside as well as
inside. Occasions may even arise when this triangular shape
of a church is needed. I have only given a rough idea of it,
but those who know about architecture can easily make up
all the details. It would cost me little effort to vary the*
ordonnance *over the same plan in five or six different ways.
Ingenious architects would be even less troubled than I to
arrange the architectural design of a church in a dignified
manner over any plan whatsoever provided it does not depart
from regular shapes.*]

Chapter V
On the Embellishment of Towns

The taste for embellishment has become widespread; it is desirable for progress in art that it lasts and improves. However, it must not be confined to private houses only, but must comprise whole towns. Most of our towns have remained in a state of neglect, confusion and disorder, brought about by the ignorance and boorishness of our forefathers. New houses have been built but neither the bad distributions of the streets nor the unsightly irregularity of the decorations, made at random and according to anybody's whim, are changed. Our towns are still what they were, a mass of houses crowded together haphazardly without system, planning or design. Nowhere is this disorder more noticeable and more shocking than in Paris. The center of this capital has hardly changed for three hundred years; there are still the same number of little, narrow and tortuous streets smelling of dirt and filth where the encounter of carriages causes constant obstruction. The outlying districts which were only inhabited much later are less badly built, but one can rightly say that, excepting some buildings here and there, Paris is, on the whole, far from being a beautiful town. Superior to all other towns through its immense size, the number and wealth of its inhabitants, it is inferior to many in those beneficial things that make a town convenient, agreeable and magnificent. Its avenues are miserable, the streets badly laid out and too narrow, the houses plain and banal, the squares few in number and insignificant and nearly all palaces badly placed—in short, it is a very big, disordered town where one encounters few striking objects and is much surprised to find nothing that is in accordance with the idea one had formed of it or that comes anywhere near to what one has seen in more than one less famous town.

Paris is therefore in great need of, and ready for, embellishment. So as to contribute the best I can to a possible project for giving Paris in time all the beauty which it has not at present, I will relate here in detail the principles on which to act and the rules which in the main one ought to follow.

The beauty and splendor of a town depends mainly on three things: its entries, its streets and its buildings.

Article I
On Entries of Towns

The entries of a town must be (1) free and unobstructed; (2) numerous, proportionate to the circumference of the wall; (3) sufficiently ornate.

The entry into a town is meant to facilitate the comings and goings of the inhabitants and strangers. In order to avoid a crowded concord it is necessary that everything is perfectly free and unobstructed. The avenue contributes much to this. By avenue I understand the roads leading to the town; the more populated the town and the greater the crowd, the wider these roads have to be. It is not enough that the avenue has the appropriate width close to the town; this width must start at a fair distance so that one need not be afraid of crowding at the gate. Lately, all the avenues of Paris have been widened, but two main crossings over the river have been omitted which at certain times are liable to abnormal crowding when the ease of access is greatly impeded. These two crossings are the bridge of Sèvres and the bridge of Neuilly. Apart from it being very improper that two bridges intended to connect the Court with Paris are only wooden bridges, undecorated and not very solid, it is highly inconvenient to find at the entrance to both a gate through which two carriages cannot pass next to each other without colliding and to have on the bridges a width hardly sufficient for the two carriages to drive along and not graze the parapet. This omission may cause serious accidents; the inconvenience is so noticeable that it is surprising that nobody thinks of rectifying it.

It is not enough that the avenue be wide and as far as possible without bend and deviation; the gate and the street inside, which corresponds to the avenue, must also have these advantages. It would even be desirable to find a large square opened up by several streets forming a fanlike pattern (*en patte d'oie*) at the entrance to a big town. The entrance to Rome at the Porta del Popolo is in this style; we have nothing like it in Paris. It would be easy to lay out the entrance to the Faubourg St. Antoine in this way, but that would be doing it at the wrong end. It would be much better to draw up a new general plan and arrange, along the lines of this idea, the two main entries to Paris at the Porte St. Martin and the Porte St. Jacques with a street in the middle to run from one end of the town to the other and with more streets on either side in a starlike pattern to connect with the main quarters and to end at some important building.

The greater the circumference of a town the more necessary it becomes to increase the number of gateways; in general there has been little failure in doing this, but not enough attention has been paid to setting them at roughly equal distances which would result in more order and greater convenience. Necessity has given rise to the great number of tollhouses which serve as entry and exit to Paris, but accident has placed them where they are with oddly unequal distances between them; this produces a very irregular and deformed surrounding wall. A more or less regular polygon should have been marked out, beyond which no expansion was to be permitted, and enforced so that nobody would take it upon himself to pass beyond the prescribed limits; once the surrounding wall was thus formed, the gates and entries of the town should have been distributed either at each face or at each angle of the polygon.

The gateway of a great town must have decor and an air of magnificence and grandeur. Nothing is more pitiful and more wretched than the tollhouses which at present are the real gates of Paris. From whichever side one arrives in this capital, this is what one sees first: some miserable palisades put up somehow on wooden planks, turning on two old hinges and flanked by two or three dunghills. This is what qualifies for the pompous title of gates of Paris. Nothing as miserable as this is to be seen in the smallest boroughs of the kingdom. Strangers who pass these tollhouses are thunderstruck when they are told: "Now you are in the Capital of France." It needs arguing to convince them; they can hardly believe their eyes; they imagine they are still in some neighboring village. All this proves how improper it is for the gates of a town like Paris to be so devoid of any sort of ornament.

Where the tollhouses now stand one should erect great triumphal arches on which the memory of the great deeds which made the reigns of our kings famous would be immortalized. Triumphal arches are the most fitting decoration for the entries of a town like Paris. They proudly announce the place of residence of the conquering monarchs who filled the whole of Europe with their exploits. People are in difficulty about setting up monuments to the glory of the august princes who govern us: which monuments could be more worthy of them than beautiful triumphal arches? They provide a simple and natural way of passing on to posterity the memory of their great actions and, when placed at the entry to the town, right away display these actions to the stranger. That is how the Romans, a nation which had only noble ideas and always thought on a grand scale, honored their emperors. They did not think of creating immensely large squares merely to place at the center of each a solitary statue of one of these rulers of the world. They marked their greatness much better by erecting on several avenues of their town superb arches which recall the military triumph, the climax of their great actions. By taking up the ideas of this admirable nation and giving to all entries into our capital this Roman air, this lofty style of decoration we shall gain a twofold advantage. We shall create magnificent entrance gates capable of attracting the attention and holding the admiration of the stranger and will, without too much cost, set up monuments which will contribute both to the glory of our kings and to the edification of posterity.

During the reign of Louis XIV, when the greatness of this monarch seemed to have exalted the ideas of all artists, one was conscious of this twofold usefulness of the triumphal arches. This has given us the Portes St. Martin, St. Denis, St. Bernard and St. Antoine. If universal good taste had at that time not come to an end or had subsequently become depraved, all our avenues to this capital would have noble decorations today.

Triumphal arches have a style of their own. They demand grandeur in proportions, simplicity and strength in ornament, something vast and bold in volume. The Porte St. Denis is in my opinion a masterpiece of its kind. Nothing is more majestic than the astonishing width and beautiful elevation of this semicircular arch, nothing more judicious than its attendant ornaments, nothing more masculine and vigorous than the statues and bas-reliefs, nothing better drawn and more boldly cut than the entablature that crowns it. I do not know any triumphal arch of ancient Rome of a composition as brilliant, noble, and lofty as this superb gateway. I could not say the same about the Porte St. Martin; its arcades are too small, its mass is too heavy and coarse and the immense labor of the vermiculated rustication only gives it a most disagreeable Gothic appearance. The Porte St. Bernard is altogether shocking. In a triumphal procession the triumphant commander must be in the center. Here, he is going to break his nose on a pier and has to turn aside to pass on the right or the left. This is an unbearable fault and greatly spoils the rest of the otherwise beautifully executed building. A triumphal arch must either have only a single arcade or otherwise three; when it cannot be very wide, one must be content with one arcade, as at the Porte St. Denis, or else be compelled to make three small openings hardly large enough for an entrance to a private house, as can be seen at the Porte St. Antoine, one of the most banal and defective pieces of architecture.

I would not follow the style of the ancient Romans, who nearly always made use of pedestals, columns, and regular entablatures on triumphal arches. According to the principles which I have established, columns and arcades can never go well together. Columns on triumphal arches always seem to be a superfluous and false ornament which can only enlarge their mass to a ridiculous degree and, if I may say so, spoil the simple, natural and slender shape of the whole work. Nothing prevents anyone from creating something beautiful and grand without recourse to an architectural system (*ordonnance*) incorporating columns; the Porte St. Denis is evident proof of it. Columns always convey the idea of a house meant to be lived in; yet a triumphal arch can only be a passage. It is therefore in accordance with the principles of truth and nature to give these monuments a different decoration. The genius of a capable man is an inexhaustible resource; by always following the particular style of this class of building, he will contrive to vary endlessly the turns and expressions of the same idea.

I imagine a great avenue, very wide and straight, lined with two or four rows of trees; it ends at a triumphal arch, similar to the one I have described; from there one enters a large place formed by a half-section of a circle, of an oval or of a polygon; several streets extend fanlike from it (*en patte d'oie*) of which some lead into the center, others to the outlying districts of the town and all with a vista of a beautiful work. All this combined will make it the most beautiful entry to a town imaginable. For a long time to come one cannot execute anything similar in a town like Paris. Too much must be pulled down, too much be rebuilt. But at least one can make the plan for it and order its execution step by step as the houses decay with age. What we will have begun, our descendants will conclude. Posterity, indebted to us for having imagined the scheme, will give us credit for a thousand masterpieces which, when executed, will recall in centuries of the most distant future the soundness and grandeur of our ideas.

Article II
On the Layout of Streets

The streets of a great town cannot make communication easy and convenient unless they are sufficiently numerous to prevent lengthy detours, sufficiently wide to forestall any obstructions and perfectly straight to shorten the way. Most streets of Paris are, on the contrary, in default of all this. There are large and much visited quarters which are connected with other quarters by one or two streets only; this regularly causes great congestion or at least makes considerable detours unavoidable. The only connection to the whole quarter St. Honoré from the Pont Neuf to the end of the Tuileries garden is by a single street and two small turnstiles. Along the whole length of the rue St. Antoine there are only two thoroughfares for carriages to drive to the river. Bridges across the river are not in sufficient number and the two districts at each end are without any. The streets are mostly so narrow that one cannot pass through them without danger and so winding and so full of senseless bends and corners that the way between one place and another becomes twice as long.

One must look at a town as a forest. The streets of the one are the roads of the other; both must be cut through in the same way. The essential beauty of a park consists in the great number of roads, their width and their alignment. This, however, is not sufficient: it needs a Le Nôtre to design the plan for it, someone who applies taste and intelligence so that there is at one and the same time order and fantasy, symmetry and variety, with roads here in the pattern of a star, there in that of a *patte d'oie*, with a featherlike arrangement in one place, fanlike in another, with parallel roads further away and everywhere *carrefours* of different design and shape. The more variety, abundance, contrast and even disorder in this composition, the greater will be the piquant and delightful beauty of the park. One should not believe that *esprit* has a place only in higher things. Everything which is susceptible of beauty, everything which demands inventiveness and planning is suitable to set off the imagination, the fire, the verve of a genius. The picturesque can be found in the pattern of a parterre as much as in the composition of a painting.

Let us carry out this idea and use the design of our parks as plan for our towns. It is only a question of measuring the area and making the same style roads into streets and *carrefours* into squares. There are towns with perfectly aligned streets, but since the plan was made by uninspired people, a boring accuracy and cold uniformity prevail which makes one miss the disorder of towns of ours that have no kind of alignment at all; everything is related to a single shape, to a large parallelogram transversed lengthwise and crosswise by lines at right angles. Everywhere we have only boring repetition of the same objects, and all quarters look so much alike that one is mistaken and gets lost. A park which was only an assemblage of isolated and uniform squares and where all roads differed only numerically would be very tedious and dull. Above all, let us avoid excessive regularity and excessive symmetry. Dwelling too long on the same sentiment will blunt it. Whoever does not vary our pleasures, will not succeed in pleasing us.

It is therefore no small matter to draw a plan for a town in such a way that the splendor of the whole is divided into an infinite number of beautiful, entirely different details so that one hardly ever meets the same objects again, and, wandering from one end to the other, comes in every quarter across something new, unique, startling, so that there is order and yet a sort of confusion, and everything is in alignment without being monotonous, and a multitude of regular parts brings about a certain impression of irregularity and disorder which suits great cities so well. To do this one must master the art of combination and have a soul full of fire and imagination which apprehends vividly the fairest and happiest combinations.

There is no other town which provides such fine scope for the inspiration of an ingenious artist as Paris. It is an immense forest varied by the contrast between plain and hill and, in the very middle, crossed by a great river which, dividing into several branches, forms islands of different sizes. Supposing the artist were allowed to slice and carve as he liked, how much he could profit from so favorable a diversity. What happy thoughts, ingenious turns, variety of expression, wealth of idea, bizarre connections, lively contrasts, what fire and boldness, what a sensational composition! It will doubtless be said that inventing the plan will be a pure loss because of the difficulty and even impossibility of executing it. Why should the thing be impossible? So many provincial towns, with meager resources, have had the courage to contemplate rebuilding the town on a new plan, hoping to achieve it with the help of time and patience. Why despair of giving Paris such a fitting embellishment? In the capital of a great kingdom like France the resources are infinite. We only need to begin; time will complete it all. The greatest projects demand only resolution and courage provided they meet no physical obstacle. Paris is already one of the greatest cities in the world. Nothing would be more worthy of a nation as bold, ingenious, and powerful as the French than to start on a new plan which in time will make Paris the most beautiful city in the universe.

Article III
On the Decoration of Buildings

When the plan of a town is well mapped out, the main and most difficult part is done. It remains, however, to regulate the exterior decoration of the buildings. If one wants a well-built town, the facades of houses must not be left to the whim of private persons. Every part that faces the street must be determined and governed by public authority according to the design which will be laid down for the whole street. It is necessary to settle not only the sites where it will be permitted to build but also the style in which to build.

The height of the buildings should be in proportion to the width of the street. Nothing is more disagreeable than buildings of insufficient height in towns where the streets are very wide. However beautiful the buildings otherwise may be, if they seem low and dwarfed there is nothing noble or even agreeable about them.

As to facades of houses, they need regularity and much variety. Long streets where all houses seem to be one single building, because one has observed a rigorous symmetrical scheme, are a thoroughly boring sight. Too much uniformity is the worst of all faults. It is therefore necessary that in the same street the facades are free of this ugly uniformity. To build a street well, uniformity is only needed for facades which correspond and run parallel. The same design should extend over a whole section which is not crossed by another street and must never be repeated in any similar section. The art of varying the design depends on the various forms given to the buildings, on the amount of ornaments applied and on the different way in which they are combined. With these three means each of which is almost inexhaustible one is able, even in the largest towns, never to repeat the same facade twice.

It would, even with variation in design, be a great fault if all the embellishing decoration were the same. The beauty of a painting consists in gradation of light which passes insensibly from the darker to lighter parts and in a sweet harmony of colors which is not at all incompatible with some bold contrasts or, rather, becomes more marked when among the complementary colors there are some which upset the tranquility through the effect of dissonance. Do we wish to decorate our streets in an exquisite style? Then we must not use ornaments in profusion; let us apply much that is simple, a little that is casual together with elegance and magnificence. As a rule one should change from the casual to the simple, from the simple to the elegant, from the elegant to the magnificent, should occasionally proceed abruptly from one extreme to the other using contrasts the boldness of which attracts the eye and produces strong effects, abandon from

131

time to time symmetry and give in to caprice and eccentricity, blend the soft with the hard, the delicate with the rough, the noble with the rustic, and never depart from the true and natural. It seems to me that in this way one can display on the different houses of a town that pleasant variety and delicate harmony that make the charm of the decoration.

Paris is large enough so that one can use all types of decoration on its buildings. Its bridges, embankments, palaces, churches, great *hôtels*, hospitals, monasteries and public buildings provide the occasion for frequent interruption of the form of ordinary houses by quite singular forms. By knocking down the dreadful hovels which overload, narrow, and disfigure most of our bridges and putting in their place beautiful large colonnades stretching from one side to the other, by facing all banks of the river and changing them into wide embankments, by lining all these embankments with facades enriched, some more, some less, by a decoration of fine gradation according to a well understood overall design, a scene will present itself from one end of the Seine to the other which will not be matched by anything in the world. Then if people, walking on both sides of the river through ingeniously laid out and perfectly aligned streets, pass in succession municipal buildings, *hôtels*, palaces, church facades and squares; if they see facades of private houses on which, with regularity preserved, the casual, the simple, the elegant and the magnificent are artistically blended and judiciously selected and set off to great advantage by contrasting one against the other; if, lastly, now and then buildings come into view of bizarre design and shape decorated in the style of the *grand pittoresque*, then I doubt that their eyes could ever tear themselves away from such a fascinating spectacle. Paris would, in its external appearance, no longer be merely an immense city, it would be a unique masterpiece, a marvel and delight. I wish that this scheme of embellishment, of which I have outlined the principles and have fixed approximate rules, would find connoisseurs who appreciate it, amateurs who favor it, devoted citizens who kindly consent to it and intrepid magistrates who seriously consider it and make efficient preparations to having it executed. I know that everything which aims at something useful has preference over that which simply intends to please. However, one can pursue the useful without neglecting the agreeable and must remember that a project which tends to give strangers a grand idea of our nation and attracts them in great numbers is a project that is not without usefulness.

Chapter VI

On the Embellishment of Gardens

Garden art has become known to us very late. Before the reign of Louis le Grand even the idea that a garden could have any other beauty than that of wild nature had not occurred to anyone. Trees, flowers, grass, and water were assembled within a great enclosure, but with so little taste and planning that nothing could have been more rustic and wild. Louis XIV was born, and hardly had the noble tastes of this lofty and sensitive mind become manifest than all arts felt the effect of his intense love for beauty. Garden art was created in France under his reign. Admirable compositions came to life under the pencil of the famous Le Nôtre in which all the beautiful things in nature, arranged in a new order and with fascinating harmony, presented the most delightful sights. Everybody was carried away by a novelty so full of genius and sentiment; it became a general ambition to substitute for dull orchards true gardens arranged with taste, adorned with grace and filled with all those delightful (*riant*) objects which until then had existed only in the poet's imagination. These changes were not brought about by tyranny of fashion, so common in France and often so dangerous. The sway of beauty alone, always invincible, can take credit for an invention the merit of which a thousand charms proclaim. Hence this multitude of enchanted places, of parterres and groves, arranged with the help of the Graces, which make the surroundings of Paris superior to Paris itself.

Garden art is perhaps the only art that has not degenerated in France. We have improved on the ideas of Le Nôtre and have in this instance successfully made use of that talent which is the most characteristic of our nation, namely not so much to invent as to correct, refine, and improve foreign inventions. Every day our gardens take on a decor that is more and more delightful, true and natural; since the object of gardens is to provide new attractions for an inclination that makes us all seek the relaxing atmosphere of the countryside, the art designed to make the stay more and more agreeable will presumably be steadily improved.

We should never lose sight of the principle so necessary and so favorable to the progress of the art—that no art has yet reached the last degree of perfection, that there is much to correct and much to add to what we call masterpieces. The question is to know the faults in which they abound and to imagine what beauty they lack; that is the only way to work for true perfection.

In gardens, one should pay particular attention to places of a delightful and simple beauty; one must make use of all the fairness nature offers and embellish its creations by arranging them in a graceful and tender manner without ever taking away from them that simple and pastoral air which makes their charm so sweet. This is what pleases us in nature: (1) the shade of the woods, the green of the meadows, the murmur of the brooks; (2) pretty viewpoints, pleasant landscapes; (3) the happy extravagance (*bizarrerie*) of nature's arrangements and that beautiful carelessness (*beau négligé*) which bars from its adornment any appearance of studied affectation. The task is to combine all these favorable features in an arrangement which allows us to sense more keenly the contrasts and harmony yet does not efface the natural and graceful.

The gardens of Versailles have for a long time been accepted by us as one of the wonders of the world and still are so among foreigners. I say of these gardens what I have already said of the Château: masterpieces are met at every step. Puget, Girardon, and many others have by their inimitable works given so much splendor to the gardens that as long as there are lovers of beauty among men they will come from all parts of the world to feast their eyes on the sight of these marvels which raise the French genius to the level of the Greek and Roman genius. But apart from this, have these gardens something that offers an agreeable and delightful spectacle for mind and eye to enjoy? One will judge this by the critical examination I am going to make. If wealth of bronzes and marbles, if nature stifled and buried under such an exaggerated display of symmetry and pomp, if a strange, extraordinary, stiff, and bombastic style makes up the beauty of a garden, then Versailles deserves to be preferred to all others. But judged by our impressions what do we find when walking in these stately gardens? At first astonishment and admiration but soon sadness and boredom. What is the reason for this disturbing impression in a place where immense sums have been spent for its embellishment? This is what ought to be examined, and we shall then notice many faults which, by depriving a garden of the delightful and graceful, deprive it of its most essential beauty.

The first fault which strikes everybody is the situation of these gardens. This narrow valley, surrounded on all sides by barren mountains and gloomy forests, is a repulsive wilderness which can only result in a wild scene. Therefore, whatever the expense, it was absolutely impossible to make good this misshapen ground. Many things had to be done in defiance of nature, and the riches that have been lavished on this garden suit it as badly as curls and pompons suit an ugly face. There will never be pleasant gardens unless places already embellished by nature are chosen, delightful places where the eye will fall on a landscape adorned with a thousand rustic charms and where comtemplation will give rise to those moments of sweet reverie which hold the soul in happy repose. Many of these beautiful situations exist around Paris, yet one had to search the woods for the loneliest and gloomiest to find that for Versailles.

[*The gardens of Marly have a somewhat more advantageous position. In front of the kind of building called the Château there is a small opening which partly discloses the grand spectacle to be seen from the terrace of St. Germain. This advantage, modest though it is, removes at least from the narrow valley of Marly the severe unpleasantness of an habitation placed in the center of thick forests. Yet, this advantage does not by far suffice to render the situation of Marly as delightful as one could wish and as, in fact, it could be. This distant and limited vista presents a spectacle which, from the little seen, gives an idea of its extent and magnificence but which, far from causing satisfaction, only serves to arouse desire and regret. One would like to have access to the unrestrained enjoyment of such an enchanting sight and is annoyed about the various obstacles which block and restrict such a beautiful view. This impatience, this uneasiness which take possession of the soul make it almost insensitive to the alluring objects which embellish this charming valley. It was easy to leave nothing to be desired in such a beautiful spot. All it needed was to change the position of the Château a little by moving it forward on the slope of the mountain close to the river. From there one would have enjoyed an admirable view, broken and unimpeded, which would have been more satisfying than at St. Germain because it would not have been so steep; one could have extended sloping gardens to the right and left and would have found again at the rear this pleasant valley by which one is now unfortunately enclosed; it would have presented a most interesting diversity. It seems, however, that Louis le Grand was not very sensitive*

137

to the attractions of beautiful situations. Versailles and Trianon prove that he did not make the effort to look for them while Marly almost proves that he preferred to avoid them. Regarding money spent, the gardens of St. Cloud are quite inferior to all those I have just mentioned but greatly surpass them by the advantage of their situation alone. The viewpoints are so artistically arranged and so happily varied that, wandering through the gardens, one passes from one delight to another, arrested at every step by the beautiful places encountered. The charm is so vivid and lasting that one leaves St. Cloud only with regret, firmly resolved to return there. At Meudon one was quite free to have gardens in a situation that would have brought about the same touching effects, but by an incomprehensible caprice things were so arranged that the beautiful view is at the side of the avenues and walks; in a place where nature offered by way of situation everything that could possibly be desired, one has managed to make the gardens almost as enclosed and wild as those of Versailles.]

The second fault of these gardens is the strict system of regularity. The grand manner of symmetry is not at all suitable for beautiful nature. There must, indeed, be selection, order and harmony but nothing which is too constricted and too formal. The *fer à cheval*, the parterres, avenues and groves are all done with a constraining accuracy very much removed from nature's pleasant carelessness and piquant *bizarrerie*. Art, far from being hidden, is evident everywhere and in every possible way, like one of those discourses, full of affectation, with every turn studied and every phrase rounded off, where all is measured by the square. This fault, still to be met with in most of our gardens, diminishes their enjoyment to such an extent that for pleasant promenades one has to leave these groves where art is too conspicuous and go and look for *la belle nature* amidst the open country adorned with artless naivete. Chinese taste in gardens is, I think, preferable to our taste. The description of the emperor's countryhouse in the *Lettres édifiantes* indicates great naivete in the decoration of their gardens. The asymmetry they are fond of, the capricious way in which they design and lay out the bosquets, canals and everything surrounding these must, because of the rustic character, be all the more attractive. Nobody can resist the charm of this description; reading it one believes one is wandering in the midst of those imaginary gardens where fairies wave their magic wands yet, on reflection, realizes that everything there is just simple and natural. The better simplicity is understood, the more will truth and nature dominate our tastes. I wish the author of the pretty description had given us the actual plan of this delightful country seat which, no doubt, could serve us as a good model. By ingeniously fusing the Chinese conceptions with ours we would succeed in creating gardens to which nature with all its charm has returned again.

[*On even ground it is very difficult to draw up a plan for a garden in which regularity and formality are joined to that pleasant disorder of which nature is so fond. On uneven ground one has many more opportunities to vary things and display ingenious carelessness. When one is fortunate enough to be able to bring together within the same enclosure hollows, high ground, more or less steep slopes, some plains in the distance and several plateaus on the hills, then one has all the variations of nature in a condensed form and a wide field for imitating its playful eccentricities. When given the choice, the man of genius will always prefer the uneven to the even ground. On uneven ground, he will find a thousand ways to invent new spectacles, form enjoyable contrasts, produce delightful surprises, avoid any kind of monotony, place everywhere something which is singular and picturesque and retain the true and natural look of everything. On level ground, on the contrary, he must force his mind not to give in to insipid symmetry; he may well have his dreams, yet will be driven to follow convention and repeat himself endlessly. Those who want gardens on level ground only look, no doubt, for convenient promenades, but they do not know what visual charm and spiritual pleasure mean.*]

A third fault of the gardens of Versailles is that one feels too much hemmed in. One goes into a garden to breathe fresh air and be at ease. Here, one always seems to be within four walls; everywhere there are masses of greenery which do not allow the eye to range freely far afield or the air to circulate. The *palissades de charmille* are real walls which because of their height and straight alignment turn an avenue into a boring street. The unpleasantness of these green walls was felt. Quite rightly one took a dislike to them and sought means by which to enjoy shade without losing the view and to escape the heat of the sun without being confined between two walls. In this one succeeded through planting trees with the trunks left free and unencumbered and the crowns joined together; they form the desired cover in a thousand different ways. Hence the charming *quinconces* which provide cool shade without obstructing the view and arcades and bowers that form a vault of greenery supported by as many columns as there are tree trunks. I do not mean that dense masses must be completely excluded; in nature many exist in forests. What I do mean is that these masses should be used sparingly since by themselves they have something dismal and wild about them. They should be used in the same way as shades are used in a painting to heighten the lights, and dissonances are used in music to underline the consonances; for there is harmony in everything. The gardens of Versailles are like the paintings of Caravaggio in which black predominates excessively or like modern music where the profusion of dissonances badly affects the senses.

A fourth fault of these gardens is the lack of bright fresh green and the arid appearance of it all. No visual sensation is as sweet as a beautiful green. If one wants to let this sensation grow into exquisite pleasure, it only needs the green to be arranged in shades ranging from a very bright to a most delicate tone. All *broderies* in the parterres of Versailles are outlined by edges of box and filled with differently colored sand and rather indifferent flowers. Nothing is more dismal and less natural than these *broderies.* I prefer a simple meadow; there, at least, I find fresh green whereas in these parterres *en broderie* my eyes get tired through seeing almost nothing but sand and the very little green of some box which is too dull to give any pleasure. The only beautiful parterres are parterres *en gazon*; they can be made up either of simple compartments or of true *broderie* and, provided the grass selected is very fine and of a bright green, they will always look satisfactory. When I say *gazon en broderie*, this is what I mean by it: a design of *broderie* of different greens, two or three shades, in the same style as certain tapestries where only one color is used ranging from the deepest to the lightest shade. In this design, I should like the flowers to be arranged in clusters and to let the gardener decide not only on the right place for these flowers but also on the particular kind of flower suitable to give an exquisite brilliance to this carpet of green embroidery. To me such a parterre would be of perfect beauty because it would combine what is most agreeable in nature with the resources art has to embellish nature itself.

[*Until now one has not thought of anything better than to sand the promenades so as to walk there comfortably and without getting dirty. Yet sand is arid and its color unsightly. However fine its quality, it always is somewhat hard underfoot. The pleasure of the promenade demands something softer. Nature has produced nothing of this kind comparable to a fine lawn; it is a tender down, a soft rest for the foot. It has none of the inconvenience of ordinary grass, never shorn short enough to walk on it comfortably, and has a particular shade of green that is pleasing to the eye. A fine lawn is the softest rug, most suitable for garden walks. Only natural lawn is known, but could it not be made artificially? Some studies on the nature of the plants of which it is composed and of the ground on which it grows would be sufficient to enable art to imitate this little marvel of nature. The thing is certainly worth the trouble.*]

In the bosquets of Versailles green is sometimes badly chosen and always badly arranged. The green of the yew tree is too gloomy and too dark. Formerly people were very fond of these pyramids of yew trees trimmed in a thousand bizarre shapes which look like the different pieces on a chess board. Good taste has done away with these ridiculous fancies, though there are still many remnants of them left in Versailles. The green of the bosquets is too uniform; there should be more variety and more order. Different trees have different shades of green. What can be more delightful, more graceful than a judicious blending of these shades producing a chiaroscuro almost as correct and as fascinating as in a beautiful painting? A gardener ought to be an excellent painter or, at least, have a good knowledge of that part of painting which has to do with complementary colors and with the different tones of the same color. He could then arrange the green so as to create surprise and enable us to enjoy unusual pleasure.

In the gardens of Versailles there is no water, and what is a garden without water? Only water can preserve the freshness of the garden, revive its beauty and give it soul and life. The murmur of running waters is good company in a solitary garden. Sitting by a fountain or a brook we can believe we watch the banter of nymphs and naiads when the ever-changing bubbling and cascading waters beguile and captivate us, speak to us and make us dream. What an amount of money has been spent to bring water to Versailles! The surrounding country has been requisitioned, the canals, the aqueducts and the Seine, raised by machines to the level of a high mountain, have all been put into action at great cost to make good the water that was completely lacking. Having spent immense sums of money on this task, all one is able to do is to pour out, with the help of an endless number of every kind of jet, two or three times a year, dirty waters which gush miraculously into the air for just a few minutes and then vanish into different channels that feed the so-called canal and the basins (*eaux plates*). The rest of the time there is not a drop of running water to be seen, only dry fountains and basins half-filled with smelly water. [*It is true that during the summer months one frequently enjoys the spectacle of the so-called* petites eaux, *and it must be admitted that the great number of basins from which abundant water issues with great noise much enlivens the dull gardens of Versailles. But it is very unfortunate that funds are not sufficient to go to the same expense every day. One is reduced to showing off on Sundays and feast days; the rest of the week things look poor; there is no question of either* grandes *or* petites eaux. *One lives in the driest place in the universe.*]

It is infinitely better to have much less spectacular water displays but to enjoy them regularly. A pretty, lively stream which in one place flows through little pools, in another rushes down in waterfalls, and further on gushes into the air, on one side trickles through the rocks of a grotto and on the other frolics in little spurts and splashes, which, in short, takes on all sorts of forms and plays all sorts of games is preferable to all the short-lived miracles of Versailles.

The critical examination I have just made of this too stately and not at all delightful garden is sufficient to give at least a vague idea of the style that should be prevalent in the decoration of any kind of garden. If, first of all, one takes care to plant greenery, to vary and blend it, if one is not subjected to the restraint of having to follow too formal and too symmetrical a design, arranges viewpoints carefully, plans thickets and clearings intelligently, distributes water over all parts of the garden and lets it run and gush forth with more or less force and abundance depending on the capacity of the source and, lastly, lays out the whole so well that there are open views, shade and freshness—then one will create truly delightful gardens.

There lives in Europe a great prince who through an exceptional run of good fortune and calamity has become famous. After a hard and troubled life providence has granted him a repose which he, a man of genius and taste, uses to advantage by devoting himself to every kind of attractive and ingenious invention. The arts are indebted to him not only for the protection he accords them, but also for enriching them by a thousand discoveries which extend the scope, vary the productions, heighten the enchantment and increase the resources of the arts. He himself gives artists the ideas, clears the way for them and presents opportunities to them with an enlightened understanding that enables even those of only moderate talent to create wonderful works. He is the first man in the world to visualize a project clearly and execute it economically and promptly. With a modest revenue he has increased his *maisons de plaisance* by a surprising number, filled them with delightful objects and adorned them with exquisite taste. There we admire the fertility of a genius who profits from everything, creates a thousand things out of nothing and adapts himself in a hundred different ways so as to offer constantly things which are new and unique and always delightful and graceful; there we see buildings of every shape which please less by rich materials than by novel design, elegant form and tasteful ornaments; there we find beauty that has the right blend of manliness and nobility with elegance and naiveté; there we walk in gardens where nature, infinitely varied, is at its best; there we see beautiful, quickly flowing waters rising as columns, plunging down in cascades, performing unique and charming displays; there we see cascades of water, halls with windows all formed by curtains of water and dining rooms illuminated by great chandeliers of water; there, in short, we find a host of ingenious novelties and everywhere it is the delightful and graceful that prevails. Let our artists attend the school of this great prince and they will learn a thousand new ways with which to surprise us, please us and enchant us.

The End

Avertissement
to the Second Edition

The good reception which the public has been kind enough to accord to this work imposes on me the obligation to neglect nothing to make it less defective. I did not hope that it would find that much favor among the many. The dry subject matter, the novelty of the principles and the boldness of the criticisms all made me fear for the fate of a book in which I dared to fight against accepted customs and prevailing prejudices with no other weapons than those of strict reasoning.

Apprehension of failure, even the wish to see my critics express their opinion without restraint made me decide from the start to let the author be unknown as his name would have added nothing to the merit of the work and could have given rise to prejudices unfavorable to him. I was fortunate to hide my identity long enough for the success of this daring work to be established before it could have been known to whom to attribute it. I expected criticisms that could have been made bluntly and was firmly resolved to profit by them. I went to search through all the periodicals to learn there of my mistakes; I found only indulgent readers who excused everything because of the integrity of my intentions.

Only recently have I learned of a work entitled *Examen*

d'un Essai sur l'architecture in which someone undertakes to prove that I have talked about an art of which I have no knowledge at all and that I have simply set up my bizarre taste and aversions as principle and rule.

This *Examen* is preceded by a foreword written differently from the rest of the work and which, I suspect, originates from a better pen. The writer treats me there in a very cavalier and offhand manner making many insulting remarks which I do not let offend me. Perhaps I would be less indifferent to solid reasons put forward against my principles than to rash imputations such as "petty genius" (*petit genie*), "half-educated" (*demi-savant*), "obscure and unknown writer," and to the exaggerated consideration which he declares to have for my youth, a man who has not seen my certificate of baptism and should have published his own. I think less sterile means must be used to make the public recover from the deception which he asserts I have imposed upon them.

The writer blames me for the boldness of my style and, above all, for the peremptory tone of what he calls my decrees. These faults, I admit, are very great but, after all, these accidental imperfections do not change anything of the substance of the matter. The question is to know whether I am on the right line or have been led astray. The author of the foreword was not commissioned to solve this problem. He merely lent his pen obligingly to a friend in need who wished to speak badly of me with some *esprit*.

I speak of the person who provided the basic material for a work in which my *Essai sur l'architecture* is examined at great length, though very superficially: I have read it with all the interest of which an author, jealous of his reputation, and a philosopher, loving truth, is capable. I easily realized that I had to do with a professional man; this made me more attentive when reading a work from which I hoped to gain much enlightenment. I found that he confronts me constantly with traditional customs, never with reasoning which could, even if only in a small way, justify them. The architect who wanted to convict me of ignorance has shown very clearly that I condemn things practiced by all masters of the art, and this I have admitted. He has, however, left out the essential thing, namely to reply to the reasons and to destroy the principles on which my criticism is based. It was of little use to write a fairly thick book to say that I lack respect for Palladio, Scamozzi, Vignola and Blondel. I have so clearly confessed to this that the public has not been deceived at all, and was by no means in need of being warned of my rashness. A page or two of good argument against my theory would have settled the problem better than those innumerable boring lamentations about the clouds with which I obscure the fame of the greatest artists.

The author of the *Examen* believes he humiliates me by incessantly repeating that all I do is to copy M. de Cordemoy who, he says, is the father of all my ideas. It is evident from what I have said in the preface and in the way I quote him on every occasion that I have no wish at all to let the reader be ignorant of the use I have made of this author in preference to all the others whom, nevertheless, I have thoroughly read. His *Traité d'architecture* contains the substance of a theory which cannot be found anywhere else. The reading of his treatise has much contributed to the development of my own ideas. But although I have profited by his learning, I believe myself to be more than a mere copyist of his views. It is easy to recognize from the manner in which I am being attacked that I am judged guilty of something more than of being the blind disciple of M. de Cordemoy.

My critic speaks on every occasion of my dislikes and gross blunders. Reading his book and thinking about it as I might I could not make out in what they consist. One of the things which he has most at heart is the obstinate war I have declared on pilasters and arches. He is not the only one to regret that I have made up my mind to proscribe them. M. l'Abbé le Blanc in his judicious *Observations sur les tableaux*, in which he praises me quite undeservedly, complains about my prejudice against such a pleasing ornament. Many others have indicated to me that this severity seems to them excessive. I myself have foreseen that people would not accept such a suppression without a murmur if only because of the rule of habit and the force of prejudice. However, I believe I have established principles which one cannot admit without necessarily deciding in favor of the suppression of pilasters and arches. It is those principles that critics must attack.

The author of the *Examen* dwells on the subject of pilasters and does not say a single word to justify their use. When, in order to refute my saying that nature makes nothing square, he confronts me with fossils and rough stones in quarries, I have nothing to answer him except that he did not understand me. It is annoying that this answer is the obvious explanation that comes to mind for most of his objections which he raises against some passages without knowing and without saying why. He agrees that the free-standing pilaster should be proscribed and would be at a loss to give a solid reason for it unless he has recourse to the principles I have established. If then the isolated pilaster must be proscribed, how is it that the engaged pilaster should find favor? These inconsistencies I do not understand at all and defy anybody to reconcile such opposites.

It is said that a practice as ancient as it is universal guarantees the good effect of the engaged pilaster. With this principle there is no abuse that could not be justified. Are the fanciful ornaments (*colifichets*) of Gothic architecture (*architecture arabesque*) less reprehensible because the whole of Europe liked them for many centuries? Are the excesses of the Cavaliere Borromini more tolerable because all Rome approved of them and because they are still copied there enthusiastically? It is essential for the success of the arts not to suffer anything that is not founded on principle; otherwise, there is no other rule than caprice.

An artist given to license (*artiste licentieux*) only needs to invent all sorts of bizarre eccentricities—no matter how much they are condemned, he will insist that they make a good effect and will cite a thousand people whom they please. No matter how strongly one argues against this view and confronts him with established rules, he will doubt that they are legitimate and reject them as arbitrary laws which have only arisen from blind routine. There is only one way to check this innovator and this is to confront him with the firm principle which he will be forced to admit and which in consequence leads directly to the condemnation of his capricious ideas.

Therefore, the architect who adores pilasters should above all go back to a definite principle from which he could draw the logical conclusion that the pilaster is legitimate. I think that intelligent readers of my *Essai sur l'architecture* have recognized that this has been my own way to proceed and that everything I called beauty, license and faults I deduced from a simple and clear principle, admitted by everybody. My adversary should not hope to get my method proscribed so long as he merely claims the habit, experience and practice of skilled people (*habiles gens*). Any of his pupils will be able to embarrass him by asking him to be good enough to give a reason for what he pronounces, saying to him: "You condemn the free-standing pilaster and want to admit the engaged pilaster, but why rather one than the other? You cite custom—but how many customs are not really abuses; experience—but how often has that been proved false; practice—but to how many irregularities has this led?" How can one get out of this impasse if not by this trick of common charlatanry? I tell you, you must believe me, and those who will tell you the opposite are ignoramuses. There is no hope

151

for progress in the arts if all is confined to imitating things already done. Criticism, which is so necessary for the perfection of the arts, can only exist once we have rules founded not on what is but on what ought to be.

I am surprised that an architect ranks the pilaster among ordinary ornaments. This is a thoughtless decision. Does he not know that what is called an ornament is an accidental adornment which one can make use of or cut out without the essence of the architectural Order being affected? Flutings and other embellishments with which the sculptor's chisel covers the various parts are true ornaments because they can be admitted or suppressed without changing the thing fundamentally. Does that apply to the pilaster? Is it not clearly an essential part of the Order making one whole with the entablature? Can one cut it out without spoiling the character of the composition? Further, it is only through an abuse that the pilaster has taken the place of the column of which it is a very inaccurate representation. The pilaster has only been invented to save the expense of columns and yet retain their general idea, but an imitation as faulty as that is no consolation for the absence of such a beautiful original. Wherever one applies pilasters there should be columns and wherever one cannot apply columns there should be no Order at all.

I should like to convince everybody of a truth in which I myself believe absolutely, namely that the parts of an architectural Order are the parts of the building itself. They must therefore be applied in such a way that they not only adorn but actually constitute the building. The existence of the building must depend so completely on the union of these parts that not a single one could be taken away without the whole building collapsing. If one imprints this reasonable and lucid principle well into one's mind one will easily recognize a host of errors arising from a practice which obstinately follows the opposite principle. No longer will these pilasters and these entablatures plastered over the solid mass of the building be taken for true architecutre; they are so much decoration only that one can destroy the whole architectural layer with a blow of a chisel without the building losing anything but an ornament. On the other hand, free-standing columns which carry an entablature never leave one in doubt about the truth of the architectural display they present because one feels that none of these parts could be touched without causing damage and ruin to the building.

Everything said in favor of twisted columns, niches and pilasters has likewise little foundation and only calls for another general examination of my principles carried out in a more mature and thoughtful manner. A great crime has been made out of the fact that I have seen pedestals at the portico of the Hôtel de Soubise where, it is said, there are none; from this the polite conclusion is drawn that I do not even know the difference between a socle and a pedestal. To accuse me of such ignorance is, I think, taking ill humor a bit far. It is clear to me that I have to do with a man who is so much slave to the routine of the workshop that he recognizes a pedestal only if there is base, die and cornice. I admit that I am not all that scrupulous about terms. Following the example of many others I call a square socle without cornice and base a pedestal, especially when it rests on another socle which alone deserves to retain this name.

Since the author of the *Examen* could not destroy my theory by true reasoning, he confronts me with practical difficulties with which he seems to be much more conversant. Objections of this kind are the only ones which I have thought of any consequence. They call for an answer from me; I shall try to make it a satisfactory one. It concerns in the first place the two stories with columns which, according to me, should be separated by a single architrave only. Against this, he raises two objections: first, that the insufficient thickness of the architrave would leave its voussoirs (*claveaux*) without the strength needed to stay in position. Second, that

the base of the upper column would project over the architrave resulting in a most shocking *porte-à-faux.*

I am very glad that my critic raises these objections. They
give me the opportunity of developing my ideas further. I
believe I have said that any portico on a first floor requires a
balustrade for support. The architect who wants to find fault
with me should not neglect to take note of this observation.
So, when placing two Orders one above the other, I always
set up the column of the upper story on a socle of a height
necessary for the balustrade, like those at the bays of the
Chapel of Versailles. Consequently, most of the feared disadvantages are overcome. Were it true, which it is not, that a
simple architrave is not thick enough to give the extrados of
the *claveaux* the width and consequently the necessary
strength, the addition of the balustrade adds a new bond
within the intercolumniations which assures solidity. This
addition also prevents the eye from being offended through
seeing the intercolumniation bridged by something as thin as
a simple architrave. Even the confusion and the alleged
entanglement pictured at the junction of lower capital, architrave and upper base do not occur.

There only remains the difficulty of the *porte-a-faux*
caused by the base and, even more, the socle projecting
beyond the architrave. Two things will rectify this faulty
projection: (1) if the columns of the upper story are, as they
should be, of a module a good deal smaller than that of the
columns below; (2) if, as I have said, one adds some moldings
to the architrave so as to obscure this projection even more. I
have suggested some; my adversary finds their contours unbearable. One should examine whether his judgment is as
sure as he thinks; if it is, one only needs to put a better
contour in the place of the one he disapproves of. One should
look for further means to eliminate a difficulty which is not
at all insurmountable and only brings oneself to use the
complete entablature when it is definitely proved that it is

impossible to do without it. Then, this imperfection would become a *licence* excusable because resorting to it is a necessity. Up to now this necessity is anything but proved.

My adversary examines my new plan of a church with great care. This is the only place where he is explicit and where he forgets insults. He attacks my idea for its lack of solidity and enters into this matter in great detail whence I shall try to follow him.

The first difficulty which occurs to him is that one column only stands at the four corners of the crossing, evidently too weak a support for carrying the weight of the vaults. This difficulty I have foreseen myself and here is how I rectify it. At the four corners of the crossing I construct four *avant-corps* meant to carry four great transverse ribs on which rests a vault *en pendentifs.* Each of my *avant-corps* consists of a group of four columns arranged in a square, that is to say I join to the one column which already stands at the corner three others; by this increase I arrive at a force sufficient to carry the vault without my ordonnance being interrupted in any way.

Objection is made that the vault of the crossing could not survive because of the impossibility of putting buttresses there. What prevents one from erecting buttresses on the wall of the aisles which run around the crossing, a wall which can be strengthened on the outside by massive piers capable of carrying the flying buttresses which are necessary to resist the thrust of this vault? In addition to all this, proportions are mentioned which I do not accept as legitimate. If I am asked for those which I would give to my church, here they are.

I fix the height of the main vaults at two and a half times the width; of the elevation I give one width to the first Order and another width to the second Order; the half width which remains makes the semicircle of my vault. From these general proportions I derive all detailed proportions. From the height which the Order should have I determine the module of my column and once this module is determined I have everything else without trouble. I give as elevation to the aisles, as to the nave, two and a half times the width; this does not leave me in any uncertainty, either about the way of spacing my columns or, consequently, about the width of my intercolumniations. Were I asked why I fix the height at two and a half times the width I would answer because I have noticed that the effect of such a height is singularly majestic. Up to the present my choice is based on no other principle than this experience. Perhaps one day, through study and reflection, I shall succeed in basing the science of proportions on more rational and firmer principles.

Up to now one went about this matter haphazardly. In a recent work, which amazes by its lavish display of engravings, the intention has been to throw light on this obscure part of the art. The author proves at length the necessity of proportions which nobody doubts, but when he should have told us in what precisely they consist, he only repeats the arbitrary opinions of some authors of the past and gives us, even more arbitrarily, musical harmonies as rule. However that may be, with my method once the height is determined all the rest is settled through a calculation which is in no way arbitrary (*libre*). From this first proportion all the others derive with certainty.

As for the plafonds of the aisles one will understand, if one recalls what I have just said about the way in which I arrange my second Order, that it is possible to make them *en creux* like those of the colonnade of the Louvre. But in case the difficulty still seems too great all one has to do is to make them flat as has been done at the great rood screen of St. Sulpice. The author of the *Examen* sets out in detail how to succeed with it. Had he always spoken so much to the point he would have clarified many things over which, instead, he tends to spread new obscurity.

He complains that in my system the aisles do not have enough width. It is true that they would only have the width of the intercolumniations which can never be excessive. But if necessary, one is free to get more room by constructing double aisles around the nave and the choir without doubling them around the crossing which does not need so much free space. My critic maintains that my barrel vault without attic would look unshapely and shocking because of the projection of the entablature. I very much doubt the correctness of this conjecture; and although I am quite aware of the fact that the vault of St. Peter's in Rome does not spring from the entablature, I am still convinced that the vault without attic could very well be a success in my system where the entablature would never be of such gigantic proportion. However, if it is thought that one should place its center somewhat above the cornice there is nothing to stop one from doing so.

One also fears that this vault would not be sufficiently lit. This could be so if, as one supposes, I placed the windows of the second story immediately over the entrance to the chapels. But I place them within the intercolumniations itself which is in the nave. When I advised raising the outer wall of the chapels by one story so as to hide the ugly spectacle of flying buttresses from view I intended to have this wall erected for the sake of exterior decoration only. I want the space in between this wall and the nave to remain empty and the buttresses and the small roofs of the aisles and chapels to be inside this open space. I said that this wall, terminated by a balustrade, should be opened up at the upper story by as many windows as are at the story below—superfluous windows, it is true, which, however, become necessary for exterior decoration and to ensure that the windows of the nave are not too much obscured.

It only remains to reply to the criticisms about my facade. However, what I have said so far contains a reply sufficient to meet the essential part of these criticisms. When my adversary blames me for allowing artists to indulge unscrupulously in all flights of their imagination I am forced to come back to my general reply and tell him that he either has not understood me or does not want to understand me.

These are the only objections of any consequence I have found in his book. It would have been better had he always confined himself to putting forward such real ones and when doing so had made an attempt not to exaggerate but to resolve them. His book would then have only been more useful and more interesting. The trouble he took in saying again and again in a hundred different ways that I am ignorant and thoughtless, a man without taste or knowledge, was quite unnecessary. No doubt he was afraid that the public might not be as willing as he wished to call my boldness by the name it deserved and wanted to arouse in them a passion for this subject which they did not have at all. I am very glad here to declare to him and all those of his profession who would like to write against me that I reply to objections but never to insults. When it shall please them to treat the matter in good faith and with fitting politeness they will always find me disposed to profit by their learning and to show them all the respect I owe to their judgments.

I am going to account in two words for the additions I have made in this new edition. The most notable is a dictionary of terms which most of my readers seemed to want. I have arranged these terms in alphabetical order; to this I have joined some plates to make them more easily understood. Throughout the book I have added explanations at many places, either to resolve difficulties which have been pointed out to me or to make points clearer which seemed to be a little obscure. Thanks to this renewed attention I hope that this edition will be less unworthy of the public's approval than the previous one.

INDEX